Teaching and Confronting Racial Neoliberalism in Higher Education

This book examines the way in which professors must confront the social implications of racial neoliberalism. Drawing on autoethnographic research from the authors' combined 100 years of teaching experience, it recognizes the need for faculty to negotiate their own experiences with race, as well as those of their students. It focuses on the experiential nature of teaching, supplementing the fields' focus on pedagogy, and recognizes that professors must, in fact, highlight, rather than downplay, the realities of racial inequalities of the past and present. It explores the ability of instructors to make students who are not of color feel that they are not racists, as well as their ability to make students of color feel that they can present their experiences of racism as legitimate. A unique sociological analysis of the racial studies classroom, this book will be of value to researchers, scholars and faculty with interests in race and ethnicity in education; diversity studies; equity; pedagogy; and the sociology of education, teaching, and learning.

Michelle D. Byng is Professor of Sociology at Temple University (Retired), USA.

Vaso Thomas is Professor of Sociology at Bronx Community College (Retired), USA.

Donna-Marie Peters is Professor of Sociology, Instructional, at Temple University, USA.

Adriana Leela Bohm is Professor of Sociology at Delaware County Community College, USA.

Mary Stricker is Professor of Sociology, Instructional, at Temple University, USA.

Routledge Research in Race and Ethnicity in Education

This series aims to enhance our understanding of key challenges and facilitate ongoing academic debate relating to race and ethnicity in education. It provides a forum for established and emerging scholars to discuss the latest debates, issues, research and theory across the field of education research that pertain to race and ethnicity.

Books in the series include:

Teaching and Confronting Racial Neoliberalism in Higher Education
Autoethnographic Explorations of the Race Studies Classroom
Michelle D. Byng, Vaso Thomas, Donna-Marie Peters, Adriana Leela Bohm and Mary Stricker

Family Engagement in Black Students' Academic Success
Achievement and Resistance in an American Suburban School
Vilma Seeberg

The Under-Representation of Black and Minority Ethnic Educators in Education
Chance, Coincidence or Design?
Christopher G Vieler-Porter

The Racialized Experiences of Asian American Teachers in the US
Applications of Asian Critical Race Theory to Resist Marginalization
Jung Kim and Betina Hsieh

British Indian Model Minority Pupils' Schooling Experiences
Attitudes, Attainment, and Strategies
Jatinder Kang

For more information about this series, please visit: www.routledge.com

Teaching and Confronting Racial Neoliberalism in Higher Education
Autoethnographic Explorations of the Race Studies Classroom

Michelle D. Byng, Vaso Thomas, Donna-Marie Peters, Adriana Leela Bohm and Mary Stricker

NEW YORK AND LONDON

First published 2024
by Routledge
605 Third Avenue, New York, NY 10158

and by Routledge
4 Park Square, Milton Park, Abingdon, Oxon, OX14 4RN

Routledge is an imprint of the Taylor & Francis Group, an informa business

© 2024 Michelle D. Byng, Vaso Thomas, Donna-Marie
Peters, Adriana Leela Bohm, Mary Stricker

The right of Michelle D. Byng, Vaso Thomas, Donna-Marie Peters, Adriana
Leela Bohm, Mary Stricker to be identified as author[/s] of this work has been
asserted in accordance with sections 77 and 78 of the Copyright, Designs and
Patents Act 1988.

All rights reserved. No part of this book may be reprinted or reproduced or
utilised in any form or by any electronic, mechanical, or other means, now
known or hereafter invented, including photocopying and recording, or in any
information storage or retrieval system, without permission in writing from the
publishers.

Trademark notice: Product or corporate names may be trademarks or registered
trademarks, and are used only for identification and explanation without intent
to infringe.

ISBN: 978-1-032-55923-0 (hbk)
ISBN: 978-1-032-58078-4 (pbk)
ISBN: 978-1-003-44244-8 (ebk)

DOI: 10.4324/9781003442448

Typeset in Times New Roman
by Apex CoVantage, LLC

We dedicate this book to all of our fellow truth-tellers. May we never stop fighting to be seen, heard and valued.

Contents

Preface *viii*

Introduction: Confronting Racial Neoliberalism
in Race Studies Courses 1

1 Feeling Race 13

2 Teaching Race 45

3 Feeling Teaching Race 74

Conclusion 96

Epilogue 102

Appendix: Methodological Reflections *106*
Index *111*

Preface

There is perhaps no workplace activity more cliché than the gathering of co-workers at the water cooler to engage in light banter, humor and more often than not, complaints about work stress or frustrations. These scenes are played out in numerous Hollywood movies, television shows and New York Times bestsellers and never fail to get a chuckle or a head nod because most of us can relate. But we are hard-pressed to find a pop culture representation of college faculty engaging in such cliché activity, with or without the water cooler. Even when faculty members are central characters in college-related movies or television shows, it seems the work experiences are usually secondary. Further, faculty lives are presented in a highly individualistic way, such that college professors are not seen "gathering" but rather are seen alone in their offices or "ivory towers." The job of a college professor is, by design, a one-person job, particularly when it comes to the classroom, but also, most often, in the case of academic research, specifically in the non-hard sciences. Not only do faculty tend to teach and research alone, but they also tend to eat alone, as, for faculty, there are no shared lunch hours, shared work hours or even necessarily shared workdays. Thus, sharing the banter, the humor and the complaining must be intentional. That is, faculty must seek one another out and exercise agency to participate in such activity.

For many years, the five of us have done just this. We have intentionally engaged each other in such banter, humor and complaining – over lunch, dinner, drinks and behind our closed office doors. While we all share the experiences of being college faculty members, we are more tightly connected by the fact that we all teach classes focused on systemic racism. It was these teaching experiences that quickly became the centerpiece of our intentional engagements. We shared readings we were excited about using in our classes, stories of students we adored or those that challenged us. We shared our fears and frustrations with the ways in which our teachings were never able to catch up with the evolving and tumultuous racial dynamics happening outside our classroom doors. This intentional engagement with others who knew "what it was like" to teach about what is arguably the most contentious social issue of

Preface ix

our society was therapeutic; it was necessary, but it certainly wasn't sufficient. That is, it wasn't enough to ease the stress, the pain and yes, often, the trauma of spending several hours each day over too many years to count, preparing and talking with young adults about the longest-running horror show in America: White Supremacy. And so, when the ASA announced in 2016 that their 2018 theme would be *racialized emotions*, we began to intentionally gather and think about how we were actually *feeling* about what we had been sharing all of these years, which led to more serious and introspective discussions about what we *felt* while in those classrooms. It turned out that despite knowing and engaging with each other for all of these years, much of what we were feeling had never been shared. Some of these feelings we hid even from ourselves. All of us knew quickly that our meetings had shifted from something cliché to something much more unique and powerful. We were ready to turn our informal discussions about the experiences of teaching Race Studies courses into formal research. What follows is the product of that research.

Introduction
Confronting Racial Neoliberalism in Race Studies Courses

Racial Neoliberalism

In August 2020, the largest public four-year university system in the country, California State University (CSU), passed a bill requiring all students to take an ethnic studies course to graduate. In light of both the massive uprisings against police brutality and the overall rise of white nationalism in and out of the White House, universities such as CSU scrambled to respond to demands coming from student and community activists that they do more than offer their solidarity in words, but in deeds as well. Yet, these courses are not new. While few universities require such classes for graduation, students across the country have been offered a plethora of ethnic/Race Studies/diversity/racism/racial stratification courses since the 1960s. And perhaps not surprisingly, research finds that these courses are often quite challenging for students both intellectually and emotionally (Haltinner 2014a). Moreover, neoliberalism/racial neoliberalism informs societal, and therein students', perceptions of the importance and persistence of race-based inequalities. For example, Kim (2016) argues that in the context of racial neoliberalism, the success of Barack Obama included – if it did not entirely depend on – the erasure of his blackness and his ability to make whites feel non-racist. The instructor of Race Studies courses is similarly situated in their relationship with their students. However, instructors of Race Studies classes, unlike President Obama, must confront the social implications of racial neoliberalism. They must, in fact, highlight, rather than downplay, the realities of institutional discrimination and the systemic racial inequalities of the past and present. However, their success as an instructor often depends on their ability to make students who are white/not Black feel that they are not racist. It also rests on the ability to make their students who are Black/not white feel that they can present their experiences with race and racism as legitimate.

This is not an easy task and one that is made even more difficult by the fact that faculty who teach Race Studies courses encounter race as an aspect of their identity and experience *and* as the subject matter of academic scholarship. For them, race is both an "object" of pedagogical inquiry and a part of their subjective experiences in and outside of the classroom. This project seeks to examine

DOI: 10.4324/9781003442448-1

2 Introduction

the simultaneity of racialized subjectivity and objectivity among college and university instructors of Race Studies classes. Specifically, we ask, *How do racialized identities inform the experiences of teaching college/university Race Studies courses within a racially neoliberal environment?* And conversely, *How does the consciousness of one's race identity combine with course content about race to impact the subjective teaching experiences of instructors?* We ask these questions within a larger framework of race and identity theories. These theories capture the complexities of race identities. They demonstrate the multitude of analytical frames that sociologists and other social scientists have brought to bear on the efforts to understand the social construction of race categories, how race is experienced by individuals, the consequences of being identified with a racial group and the implications of race-based social policies. The classic sociology of race and ethnic relations is centered on the telling of white ethnic group histories of inclusion and incorporation into white Anglo-Saxon Protestantism (Gordon 1964; Park 1964). Acknowledging the histories of legislated subordination and inequality of those with Native American and African ancestry as well as immigration exclusions and numerical limits for those of Latin and Asian descent, expands the lens of sociological analyses to include systemic discrimination. Theories that address systemic and legislated racial inequalities shift the sociological foci to institutionalized practices that reproduce white racial dominance and not-white racial subordination normatively and discursively (Bonilla-Silva 2017; Feagin 2013; Omi and Winant 1994). This work ushered in a transition in emphasis from patterns of race/ethnic group inclusion and incorporation that vary along a continuum from assimilation and cultural pluralism in relation to white Anglo-Saxon Protestantism to the analysis of racism and racial inequalities as institutionally perpetuated and discursively legitimated.

Critical theorists expand sociological analyses of race identities and racism to include discursive practices that reinforce the naturalization of race (Pagliai 2011) by highlighting the dimensions of racialization via the raced body, the racial category and subscribed subordination (Gotanda 2011). Reading race or the explicit labeling of people and practices with race terms exposes the subjective character of racialization as well as the imposed quality of racial hierarchy (Chun 2011).

Just as Civil Rights and Anticolonial movements sought to extend the protections of the liberal state to those who were not white, neoliberalism constructed what Goldberg (2008) refers to as "the traffic-cop state" that privatized everything except the security state apparatus. In other words, neoliberal policies secured private interests against the new claimants to state protections and resources. The principles of equality before the law and so on removed the state from discriminatory action while placing the consequences of such actions within the private sphere (private preferences) beyond its reach. A racialized moral economy gave rise to a racialized political economy where white privilege is not recognized or eliminated because it is a part of the social contract

Introduction 3

(Mills 2008, 1393). In other words, race as a category is not a significant social force because individualism is the ability of each person to exercise formal legal rights (Giroux 2003). That is, there is the racist ideology, and there is no institutional racism. "Hence, neoliberal racism provides the ideological and legal framework for asserting that since American society is now a meritocracy, government should be race neutral, affirmative action programs should be dismantled, civil rights laws discarded, and the welfare state eliminated" (Giroux 2003, 201). This is the framework that our students enter our classrooms with, classrooms where racial identities take center stage.

Although sociologists have addressed racism, racialization and race-based social inequalities as elements of social structure that have implications for individuals and groups, social construction and intersectionality are key concepts in the sociological understanding of identity as it relates to race and other socially salient identity categories. The core principle of social construction theory is articulated by the Thomas Theorem: "If a person perceives a situation as real, it is real in its consequences" (Thomas 1928). Other classic sociological principles and dictums are similar. For example, social meanings are imbedded in and emerge from human interactions (Blumer 1969); from symbolic interactionism, meaning is created and recreated in the processes of human interactions and, in social contexts, shared meanings inform the actions of those who are involved (Cooley 1902; Mead 1913). Further, there is the concept of the "looking glass self" where individuals come to understand their identity and its social implications through their interactions with others (Cooley 1902). On this foundation, social construction theory proposes that collectives or groups are social artifacts that are created, recreated and mobilized in a social-historical context. They rely on the cultural scripts and power relationships of their society and times. Moreover, group-based symbolic boundaries must be socially recognized to be relevant. The shared meanings that are associated with symbolic group boundaries create structural opportunities and barriers that signal their social meaning and relevance (Berger and Luckman 2011). In other words, identity is a social construction that results from social processes that take place in human interactions (Lawler 2001).

Intersectionality captures the multiplicity of identity categories that influence the experiences of individuals and groups. However, the analytical agenda of intersectional analysis concerns social inequality and power relationships (Collins 1990; Collins and Bilge 2016). What intersectionality does or reveals is the simultaneity of advantages and disadvantages in social interactions across social divisions (e.g., race, gender, age, citizenship). It uncovers culturally based patterns of fairness and inequality, extending beyond social class, embedded in how social institutions shape and solve social problems (Collins and Bilge 2016). As an analytical tool, intersectionality demonstrates that social inequalities are caused by multiple factors that coalesce around identity categories. Social power coalesces around multiple domains (i.e., structural, cultural, disciplinary and interpersonal) that inform society and social

4 *Introduction*

phenomena (Collins 1990; Collins and Bilge 2016). Through the *both-and* analytical framework, intersectionality captures relationality and interconnections across social phenomena (Collins 1990). As a concept and an analytical tool, intersectionality allows for the contextualization of social relationships, from power to inequalities, as they operate across social domains (e.g., structural, cultural, disciplinary, interpersonal), thereby revealing the complexity of social phenomena and interactions (Collins and Bilge 2016).

These theoretical perspectives address the complexity of social interactions, the long history of the social salience of racialized identities and the persistence of race-based social inequalities. It is on this foundation that college and university instructors enter classrooms to teach their students about race in the United States. The conundrum is that each instructor takes their racial consciousness with them into the classroom, as do their students. The problem is that, as instructors, we cannot divorce ourselves in the act of teaching from the experiential reality of our own race identities or the race of others. Nor can our students. Our classrooms become sites of race-based identity labor and management as we attempt to teach about a social phenomenon where the boundary between objectivity and subjectivity is simultaneously bright, blurred and invisible. Teaching and learning become sites of negotiating spoken and unspoken social rules that rely on deep and surface acting that move beyond performance to experience. Emotions are regulated and feelings are managed on the foundations of culture, social structure and institutional setting. For the instructor, the labor of teaching moves along a continuum from neutrality to burn-out. For the students, the continuum includes resistance and rule-breaking. And, yet, it is possible for the two, students and teachers, to switch positions. The destabilizing elements are pillars, from stratification to violence, that inform racism and racialized phenomena. Moreover, the emotional implications of race are present even when the topic of the lecture or discussion is about diversity, inclusion and acceptance.

Teaching Race Studies Courses: Faculty, Student, Institutional Identity

According to Mariscal (2014), colleges and universities are somewhat resistant to courses and anti-racism efforts that challenge the overarching climate of the institution. Cazenave (2014) argues that institutional resistance is heightened when courses center on white racism and systemic racism. Yet institutional concern, if not resistance, is a factor even when courses are offered that address race identities, racism and associated race-based social inequalities (Mariscal 2013). Moreover, teachers' race identities and experiences are brought with them into the classroom, thereby influencing everything that they do in that context, from deciding how to organize course content to their evaluation of students' performance (Wysocki 2013). However, when teachers present the facts of racial inequalities in neutral terms that do not highlight how racism

Introduction 5

informs experiences and quality of life, students' understanding of the societal and lived experiences created by racism is limited (Bell 2013). In other words, how faculty and students are positioned in reference to the content and structure of race studies courses informs how teachers are evaluated and how students respond to the materials. This has implications for how shared and divergent identities between teachers and their students inform learning.

Faculty identities, namely racial and gender, have a significant impact on their classroom experiences. Women faculty and faculty of color face unique challenges that lead to a higher likelihood of receiving negative evaluations from students (Harlow 2003; Tuitt et al. 2009; Pittman 2010a; Matias, Henry and Darland 2017). Women faculty of color at predominantly white institutions are especially likely to face what Pittman (2010b) describes as an oppressive classroom environment that includes students' questioning of their authority, competency and expertise as well as intimidation. Responding to these circumstances effectively amounts to an increase in their workload in comparison to their male and white peers (Kardia and Wright 2004). Moreover, students' questioning of the authority and credibility of women faculty and faculty of color impacts their ability to develop their effectiveness as instructors (Harlow 2003). In other words, they expend additional effort developing resources and practices to establish their effectiveness as instructors. Women faculty, both white and not white, are faced with managing microaggressions, including challenges to their authority that are less likely to be experienced by white male faculty. That women faculty are unlikely to be provided with resources that are either related to their unique classroom experiences or that informs their lives both inside and outside of the classroom (Kardia and Wright 2004).

The challenges faced by not white and women faculty are exacerbated when teaching Race Studies courses. Kardia and Wright (2004), for example, found that while all faculty teaching "identity based" courses are much more likely to experience student challenges to their authority, the likelihood for women faculty was even higher. Moreover, women faculty of color experienced *twice* as much pushback from students as white women faculty. Pittman (2010a) has demonstrated that women faculty of color at large, predominantly white institutions are likely to not only experience challenges to their authority but questioning of their competency, disrespect for their scholarly expertise and be the targets of threatening and intimidating behavior from white male students. Moreover, women and women faculty of color received insufficient resources for coping with identity-based challenges. They were subject to reduced recognition and rewards regarding their teaching, and they found their workplace environments to be unsupportive. Additionally, Truong (2014) found that among graduate students in a co-taught Critical Race Theory (CRT) course, the authority of women faculty of color was subordinated to that of men faculty of color. Clearly, when teaching Race Studies courses, faculty identity matters. Much of that significance interacts with the identities of their students and their institutions.

6 *Introduction*

In addition, it is important to note that due to the subject matter, students of color are likely to experience a great deal more emotional vulnerability than white students, despite or perhaps because of, the latter's heightened resistance to such material (Froyum 2013). This vulnerability, both for students of color and for faculty of color, is accompanied by their experiences of marginalization at predominantly white institutions (Harlow 2003; Tuitt et al. 2009; Pittman 2010a). The racial climate at these institutions often parallels white students' resistance that faculty teaching Race Studies courses experience in the classroom (Mariscal 2013). Additionally, there is evidence of institutional resistance to what is perceived as "radical" racial justice materials at HBCUs (Spencer 2018). Needless to say, the experience of teaching Race Studies courses translates into unique, situationally informed, experiences for faculty.

Teaching Race Studies Courses: Faculty Racialized Subjectivities

Initially, our conversations about our teaching experiences came about organically and had no purpose other than camaraderie. When we decided to be more intentional and to organize a research project about teaching Race Studies courses, themes emerged in our initial conversations that seemed to be informed by our race identities and, in some cases, were common for those of us who had the same race identity. However, some themes were *not* so consistent with race. Although race identities are social constructions (Miles 1982; Omi and Winant 1994), they are subjectively experienced (hooks 1994). As sociologists, we recognize that race and racial identity constructions are objectively consequential societally as well as for groups and individuals (Feagin and Sikes 1994; Bonilla-Silva 2017). And yet, the more we spoke, the more we began to see each other's unique subjectivities even though we had spent our professional careers teaching young adults about the socially relevant objective realities that emerge because of race identities and the associated realities of racism. This led us, given our sociological frameworks, to dig deeper into our own autobiographies/ethnographies of race both inside *and* outside of the classroom. It led us to the reality that we could not fully understand the former without the latter. We needed to explore the construction of our racial selves (our subjective foundation of *Feeling Race*) so that we could understand our racialized subjectivities in the classroom (*Feeling Teaching Race*). Moreover, we had to acknowledge the objective framing of knowledge production and the intellectual agendas of the teaching profession (*Teaching Race*). We sought to understand not just our common experiences but our divergent ones as well. We had to step back and acknowledge our own racialization (*Feeling Race*) as well as our intellectual knowledge of racism (*Teaching Race*) in order to expose the bridge between the two (*Feeling Teaching Race*). This led us to autoethnography.

Introduction 7

Researching Teaching Race Studies Courses: Autoethnographic Research Method

For much of the 1970s and 1980s, sociology remained tethered to the positivist tradition, seeking research objectivity, generalizability and separation of researcher from research subjects. It wasn't until the 1990s that the discipline of sociology began to look toward the self in its exploration of researchers' subjectivity and lived experience, in contrast to epistemological assumptions of objectivity and rational choice. Feminism and postmodernism informed the increasing turn inward as well as the increasing respect for qualitative research overall. In 1992, sociologist Shulamit Reinharz published *Feminist Methods in Social Research*, which was followed by Norman Denzin's 1994 *Handbook of Qualitative Research* and the establishment of the journal *Qualitative Inquiry* in 1995. In that same year, sociologist Carolyn Ellis published the book *Final Negotiations* about her relationship with her dying husband. While Ellis referred to her book as "experimental ethnography," it soon became a foundational work in the growing interest in what we now know as autoethnography and posed a direct challenge to methodological conventions, seeking to bring together, rather than pull apart, sociology from the humanities.

Autoethnography combines autobiography and ethnography. It seeks to place the researcher in the research site, thereby making the researcher present in the analysis. Therefore, unlike other research methods, the researcher is visible in the development and presentation of findings and conclusions (Poulos 2021). As with traditional ethnography, autoethnography is grounded in fieldwork. Yet, the method expands the definition of the field to include the experiences and reflections of the researcher. In other words, autoethnographic methods emphasize the subjectivity and the lived experiences of the researcher. The method demands a level of introspection and reflexivity from the researcher that is not found in other social science research methodologies. However, the use of personal experience does not, in and of itself, make for an autoethnography (Adams and Herrmann 2020). The method's foundation is ethnography, the placing of the researcher in a social setting that informs experience and thereby frames the analysis.

Autoethnography is a multi-layered research method that frames aspects of personal experiences with cultural and social phenomena. It captures the researcher's negotiation, acceptance, resistance and rejection of experiences, thereby weaving together the cultural, the social and the personal (Ellis, Adams and Bochner 2010). The focus of autoethnographic research varies along a continuum between the evocative and the analytic. Evocative autoethnography seeks to blend academic writing styles with narrative, dialogue and, in some cases, fiction to develop a "thick description" of the researcher's lived experiences that will evoke deep feelings of connection between the researcher and the reader (Geertz 1973). According to Ellis (1997), evocative autoethnography reveals cultural patterns and interpretations that are often obscured,

8 *Introduction*

thereby exposing experiences and phenomena that make *our lives* meaningful. In some cases, autoethnographers tell their stories and describe their private troubles to *evoke* emotions in the reader. Emotions serve as a foundation that allows the reader to understand and connect with the autoethnographic account of the researcher (Ellis 1997). On the other hand, analytic autoethnography adheres more closely to the classic research agenda of theory development. In this case, the visibility of the researcher in the autoethnographic account serves to define how the researcher is positioned in the research process as well as how findings are produced and framed. According to Anderson, analytic autoethnography is "research in which the researcher is (1) a full member of the research group or setting, (2) visible as a member in published texts, and (3) committed to developing theoretical understandings of broader social phenomena" (2006, 373). Anderson (2006) identified five features of analytic autoethnography: (1) complete member – researcher status (CMR), (2) analytic reflexivity, (3) narrative visibility of the researchers, (4) dialogue with informants beyond the researcher, and (5) commitment to theoretical analysis. Incorporating evocative and analytic autoethnographic methods in research projects allows researchers to weave together the theory that is embedded in an autobiographical/ethnographic account with the emotive aspects of the account (Williams and Jauhari bin Zaini 2016). In other words, the theory embedded in the autoethnographic account is not distinct or able to be separated from the story told by the account (Fleming and Nicholson 2013; Hayler 2013; Tedlock 2021; Gingrich-Philbrook 2016; Winkler 2018). Autoethnography lends itself to braiding together or showing and telling the emotional experience and the theoretical account simultaneously (Sparkes 2020). Analytic reflections on experiences and the emotions that they engender aid the reader in understanding the perspective and analysis of the author/researcher.

Collaborative autoethnography (CAE) takes the method and its intellectual agendas a step further by bringing together a group of researchers who pool "their stories to find some commonalities and differences" in order to "discover the meaning of their stories in relation to the sociocultural context" (Chang, Ngunjiri and Hernandez 2016, 17). The core methodologies (autobiography and ethnography) and intellectual process (self-reflexivity) are expanded to allow researchers to recognize commonalities and differences across their experiences (Chang, Ngunjiri and Hernandez 2016). Each team member brings their critically dialogic perspective as well as their active engagement in creating meaning and constructing values to the research. This effectively expands and enhances the foundation for meaning-making and analysis that results from the dialogue that takes place among the CAE members (Chang, Ngunjiri and Hernandez 2016). Each group member works individually to engage in personal meaning-making and interrogation. The group provides the context for examining the voice, experiences and perspectives of members. It is the site for questioning and prodding that adds depth to the personal interrogations of individual members (Chang, Ngunjiri and Hernandez 2016). The diversity of

Introduction 9

member experiences and perspectives enhances the analysis of the sociocultural phenomena at the heart of the research. Collaborative autoethnography is an iterative rather than a linear process. The iterative process, in combination with researcher collaboration, is the foundation for the reliability and validity of findings.

The next three chapters emerge from what we think of as a "both-and" collaborative autoethnography. Our methodology is both evocative and analytic, as well as collaborative. That is, we hope to both evoke an emotional response and push racial theory to further consider the ways in which today's racial neoliberalism is experienced in the subjective realm. Further, it must be said that the methodological attention to the way we "feel race" inherently evokes an array of emotional responses amongst the researchers that are then translated through our writing. If the reader doesn't emotionally respond to our affective explorations, one could suggest the reader is emotionally stunted! Our research is also collaborative. Collaborative autoethnography brings autoethnographic work in line with concerns about reliability and validity that legitimate research findings because the collaborative method balances the interpretative lens of individual researchers participating in the project. Researchers read, question, challenge, modify, enhance and substantiate each other's work (See Appendix for more about this process). Collaborative autoethnography allows for an organic development of Anderson's second analytic feature, "analytic reflexivity," because in these interactions with one another we are compelled to examine our thoughts and choices in bringing forth our data.

References

Adams, Tony E., and Andrew F. Herrmann. 2020. "Expanding Our Autoethnographic Future." *Journal of Autoethnography* 1 (1): 1–8. https://doi.org/10.1525/joae.2020. 1.1.1.

Anderson, Leon. 2006. "Analytic Autoethnography." *Journal of Contemporary Ethnography* 35 (4): 373–95. https://doi.org/10.1177/0891241605280449.

Bell, Joyce M. 2013. "The Importance of a Race-Critical Perspective in the Classroom." In *Teaching Race and Anti-Racism in Contemporary America: Adding Context to Colorblindness*, edited by K. Haltinner, 25–34. New York, NY: Springer Publishing.

Berger, Peter L., and Thomas Luckmann. 2011. *The Social Construction of Reality: A Treatise in the Sociology of Knowledge*. New York, NY: Open Road Media.

Blumer, Herbert. 1969. *Symbolic Interactionism: Perspective and Method*. Englewood Cliffs, NJ: Prentice-Hall.

Bonilla-Silva, Eduardo. 2017. *Racism Without Racists: Color-Blind Racism and the Persistence of Racial Inequality in the United States*. Lanham: Rowan and Littlefield Publishers.

Cazenave, N.A. (2014). Teaching About Systemic White Racism. In: Haltinner, K. (eds) Teaching Race and Anti-Racism in Contemporary America. Springer, Dordrecht.

Chang, Heewon, Faith Ngunjiri, and Kathy-Ann C. Hernandez. 2016. *Collaborative Autoethnography*. London: Routledge.

10 *Introduction*

Chun, Elaine W. 2011. "Reading Race Beyond Black and White." *Discourse & Society* 22 (4): 403–21. https://doi.org/10.1177/0957926510395833.

Collins, Patricia Hill. 1990. *Black Feminist Thought: Knowledge, Consciousness, and the Politics of Empowerment*. Boston, MA: Unwin Hyman.

Collins, Patricia Hill, and Sirma Bilge. 2016. *Intersectionality*. 1st ed. Malden, MA: Polity Press.

Cooley, Charles Horton. 1902. *Human Nature and the Social Order*. New York, NY: C. Scribner's Sons.

Ellis, Carolyn. 1995. *Final Negotiations: A Story of Love, Loss and Chronic Illness*. Philadelphia: Temple University Press. Project MUSE.

———. 1997. "Evocative Autoethnography: Writing Emotionally About Our Lives." In *Representation and the Text: Re-Framing the Narrative Voice*, edited by W. G. Tierney and Y. S. Lincoln, 116–39. Albany, NY: SUNY Press.

Ellis, Carolyn, Tony E. Adams, and Arthur P. Bochner. 2010. "Autoethnography: An Overview." *DOAJ: Directory of Open Access Journals* (November). https://doaj.org/article/be64f48522e74cadba03b10a6794cb90.

Feagin, Joe R. 2013. *The White Racial Frame: Centuries of Racial Framing and Counter Framing*. New York, NY: Routledge.

Feagin, Joe R., and Melvin P. Sikes. 1994. *Living with Racism: The Black Middle-Class Experience*. Boston, MA: Beacon Press.

Fleming, Dan, and Shaun Nicholson. 2013. "The Contact Sheet: Combining Evocative and Analytic Modes into Visual Autoethnography of the Moment." In *40th Anniversary of Studies in Symbolic Interaction*. Bingley: Emerald Group Publishing Limited.

Froyum, Carissa M. 2013. "Dealing with Emotions in the Classroom." In *Teaching Race and Anti-Racism in Contemporary America: Adding Context to Colorblindness*, edited by K. Haltinner, 81–90. New York, NY: Springer Publishing.

Geertz, Clifford. 2017. "Thick Description: Towards an Interpretive Theory of Culture." In *The Interpretation of Cultures*. New York, NY: Basic Books. First published 1973.

Gingrich-Philbrook, Craig. 2016. "Autoethnography in an Almond Grove: Uprooting the Distinction Between the Analytic and Evocative." *International Review of Qualitative Research* 9 (1): 11–28. https://doi.org/10.1525/irqr.2016.9.1.11.

Giroux, Henry A. 2003. "Public Pedagogy and the Politics of Resistance: Notes on a Critical Theory of Educational Struggle." *Educational Philosophy and Theory* 35 (1): 5–16.

Goldberg, David E. 2008. "Racisms Without Racism." *Publications of the Modern Language Association of America* 123 (5): 1712–16. https://doi.org/10.1632/pmla.2008.123.5.1712.

Gordon, Milton. 1964. *Assimilation in American Life*. New York, NY: Oxford University Press.

Gotanda, Neil. 2011. "The Racialization of Islam in American Law." *Annals of the American Academy of Political and Social Science* 637 (1): 184–95. https://doi.org/10.1177/0002716211408525.

Haltinner, Kristen. 2014. *Teaching Race and Anti-Racism in Contemporary America: Adding Context to Colorblindness*. New York, NY: Springer Publishing.

Harlow, Roxanna. 2003. "'Race Doesn't Matter, but . . .': The Effect of Race on Professors' Experiences and Emotion Management in the Undergraduate College Classroom." *Social Psychology Quarterly* 66 (4): 348. https://doi.org/10.2307/1519834.

Introduction 11

Hayler, M. 2013. "When We Got to the Top of Elm Grove." In *Contemporary British Autoethnography*, edited by N. P. Short, L. Turner, and A. Grant, 17–32. Rotterdam, The Netherlands: Sense Publishers.

hooks, Bell. 1994. *Teaching To Transgress: Education as the Practice of Freedom*. London: Routledge.

Kardia, Diana B., and Mary C. Wright. 2004. "Instructor Identity: The Impact of Gender and Race on Faculty Experiences with Teaching." Occasional Paper. University of Michigan Center for Research on Learning and Teaching. https://journals.sagepub.com/doi/10.1177/0092055X10370120?icid=int.sj-full-text.similar-articles.1.

Kim, Janine Young. 2016. "Racial Emotions of the Feeling of Equality." *University of Colorado Law Review* 87: 438–96.

Lawler, Edward E. 2001. "An Affect Theory of Social Exchange." *American Journal of Sociology* 107 (2): 321–52. https://doi.org/10.1086/324071.

Mariscal, Jorge. 2014. "How Diversity Trumped Race at One Elite University." In *Teaching Race and Anti-Racism in Contemporary America: Adding Context to Colorblindness*, edited by Kristen Haltinner, 241–47. New York, NY: Springer Publishing.

Matias, Cheryl E., Allison Henry, and Craig Darland. 2017. "The Twin Tales of Whiteness: Exploring the Emotional Roller Coaster of Teaching and Learning about Whiteness." *Taboo: The Journal of Culture and Education* 16 (1). https://doi.org/10.31390/taboo.16.1.04.

Mead, George Herbert. 1913. "The Social Self." *Journal of Philosophy, Psychology, and Scientific Methods* 10: 374–80.

Miles, Robert. 1982. *Racism and Migrant Labour: A Critical Text*. London: Routledge and Kegan Paul.

Mills, Charles W. 2008. "Racial Liberalism." *Publications of the Modern Language Association of America* 123 (5): 1380–97. https://doi.org/10.1632/pmla.2008.123.5.1380.

Omi, Michael, and Howard Winant. 1994. *Racial Formation in the United States: From the 1960s to the 1990s*. New York, NY: Routledge.

Pagliai, Valentina. 2011. "Unmarked Racializing Discourse, Facework, and Identity in Talk About Immigrants in Italy." *Journal of Linguistic Anthropology* 21 (August): E94–112. https://doi.org/10.1111/j.1548-1395.2011.01099.x.

Park, Robert. 1964. *Race and Culture*. New York, NY: Free Press.

Pittman, Chavella T. 2010. "Exploring How African American Faculty Cope with Classroom Racial Stressors." *Journal of Negro Education* 79 (1): 66–78. https://eric.ed.gov/?id=EJ943002.

Poulos, Christopher J. 2021. *Essentials of Autoethnography*. Washington, DC: American Psychological Association E-Books. https://doi.org/10.1037/0000222-000.

Sparkes, Andrew C. 2020. "Autoethnography: accept, revise, reject? An evaluative self reflects." *Qualitative Research in Sport, Exercise and Health* 12(2), 289–302. DOI: 10.1080/2159676X.2020.1732453

Spencer, Zoe. 2018. "Black skin, white masks: negotiating institutional resistance to revolutionary pedagogy and praxis in the HBCU." In *Black Women's Liberatory Pedagogies: Resistance, Transformation, and Healing Within and Beyond the Academy*, 45–63. Springer.

Tedlock, Barbara. 2021. "Introduction: Braiding Evocative with Analytic Autoethnography." In *Handbook of Autoethnography*, edited by Tony E. Adams, Stacy Holman Jones, and Carolyn Ellis, 358–510. Routledge.

Thomas, William I., and Dorothy Thomas. 1928. *The Child in America: Behavior Problems and Programs*. New York, NY: Knopf.

12 *Introduction*

Truong, Kimberly A., Daren Graves, and Adrienne J. Keene. 2014. "Faculty of Color Teaching Critical Race Theory at a PWI: An Autoethnography." *Journal of Critical Thought & Praxis* 3 (2). https://doi.org/10.31274/jctp-180810-42.

Tuitt, Frank, Michele D. Hanna, Lisa M. Martinez, María Del Carmen Salazar, and Rachel Alicia Griffin. 2009. "Teaching in the Line of Fire: Faculty of Color in the Academy." *Thought and Action* (January): 65–74. https://eric.ed.gov/?id=EJ930465.

Williams, J. Patrick, and Muhammad Kamal Jauhari bin Zaini. 2016. "Rude Boy Subculture, Critical Pedagogy, and the Collaborative Construction of an Analytic and Evocative Autoethnography." *Journal of Contemporary Ethnography* 45 (1): 34–59.

Winkler, Ingo. 2018. "Doing Autoethnography: Facing Challenges, Taking Choices, Accepting Responsibilities." *Qualitative Inquiry* 24 (4): 236–47. https://doi.org/10.1177/1077800417728956.

Wysocki, Nicholas P. 2013. "Experiencing Racialization: Digital Ethnography and Professional Development for Teachers." In *Teaching Race and Anti-Racism in Contemporary America: Adding Context to Colorblindness* edited by Kristin Haltinner, 2223–30. New York, NY: Springer Publishing.

1 Feeling Race

The Civil Rights Movement is the social backdrop that informs the development of our racial consciousnesses. It is the period of our moving into adolescence and the promises of young adulthood. More importantly, it is the period when the implications of white racial dominance and not-white racial subordination are recognized and challenged. Societally, there is an awareness of race (e.g., race identities, race relationships, race-based social inequalities) that is palpable.

We were caught in a whirlwind of rapid social change, even if the foundations of race-based inequalities were stable. For example, school integration opened the doors of educational opportunities for racial minorities even though "white flight" from the surrounding neighborhoods would follow. It was possible for Black and other not-white children to find themselves in classrooms of white students where they had no racial peers. Yet, the opening of the doors of colleges and universities would provide racial minorities with opportunities for social class mobility.

This is the context that frames our experiences of "feeling race." Our awareness of race is framed by and based on our racial identities. The variations in our identities inform our experiences, given the social salience of race in our society. At the same time, we are all aware of the social boundaries that inform race identities. We are all conscious of the social meanings, assumptions and implications of race identities for experiences. These experiences are the foundation of feeling race.

Adriana

My parents dedicated their lives to creating strong, resistance-oriented communities wherever they lived, from Massachusetts, to India, to Delaware. When I was young, I remember my parents telling me I was a child from the Third World and embedding the principles of Kwanzaa in me, pressing upon me the importance of Kujichagulia: self-determination; Ujima: collective work and responsibility; and Nia: purpose.

DOI: 10.4324/9781003442448-2

14 Feeling Race

Figure 1.1 Che'-Lumumba Students, Adriana in white hat, 1979–1980

They modeled a constant "fight for your rights" lifestyle, regardless of where we lived. I was intentionally taught revolutionary theory and instructed to challenge and resist injustice. My cultural background, early exposure to the Black Power Movement in elementary school, and parent's organizing activities shaped me profoundly. By the third grade, I was confident, outspoken and well-read on Assata Shakur, Toussaint Louverture, Angela Davis, Nat Turner, Denmark Vasey and countless others.

When we moved to Delaware in 1980, however, I also learned to be afraid. My fear revolved around many things, including violence, uncertainty and whiteness. Feeling race, in that process, shifted for me. I vacillated between being confident and proud of my Brownness to, at times, feeling scared and unsure in the face of whiteness. It was almost as if I was multiple people at once.

In the following six sections, I will highlight how I came to "feel race" in Amherst, Massachusetts; Karnataka, India; Wilmington and Newark, Delaware; Elkton, Maryland; and Catonsville, Maryland.

Amherst, Massachusetts

Growing up in Amherst, Massachusetts, our house was filled with people of different races organizing against racism, planning demonstrations and boycotts,

Feeling Race 15

laughing, yelling, theorizing and figuring out how to center racism and resistance in the classes they taught. Our house was also permeated by loud music – jazz, rock and roll, the blues. My dad loved Gill Scott Heron, Nina Simone, Billie Holiday, Elvis Presley, Carmen McRae, the Temptations, Diana Ross and the Supremes, Bruce Springsteen, Aretha Franklin, Miles Davis, etc. A Vietnam War-era veteran, anti-racist organizer, young father, and a man married to an Indian woman against his family's wishes, my dad was a trail blazer on many fronts and fought internal and external battles daily.

My mother complimented him, and was always a "main attraction." They both drew a crowd. My mom stood out for many reasons. She cooked – curried rice, red beans, chocolate cake, greens, chana masala – and no one had ever had Indian food like hers. People came in droves to eat at our house. She also liked to party. A small, petite, South Indian carpenter who wore sarees and overalls, she liked to laugh, drink and curse. In her bindi, jeans, brown skin and long black hair, she was mesmerizing.

In addition to the food and music, we also had people living with us and sharing our space on a regular basis. Titi Jamila, a "Black Puerto Rican," was from Co-Op City, the Bronx. She took me to see the Rockettes on a weekend trip to NYC in the late 1970s, and we went back to stay in the Bronx multiple times. Then there were Jane and Jill, who took me to late-night concerts. There was a woman named Lisa who taught us how to mold the fresh clay that we got down at the riverbank in Belchertown. There were Eshu and Mauricio – two young revolutionaries who were committed to raising young freedom fighters; Sonia and Angel, who had children my age – their daughter Alicia was my best friend for years; Carlie and Gary and Eric and Laura – our neighbors and extended family; Lucia and her son, Ben; Patti and her daughter Cheray. The list goes on and on. These folks created a community in Amherst, Massachusetts, where they worked super hard fighting institutionalized racism and classism on an everyday basis and taught us to be activists.

Remembering my early childhood, I realize I do not have any memories of our house being empty, of people not talking about racism and oppression, or being around one racial group. My parent's activism existed within the context of a strong collective-based community filled with other like-minded people, people who were race-conscious, identified strongly with third-world nationalism and anti-colonialism movements, and were vociferous in identifying injustice, calling it out, and building different and more equitable institutions, such as the Che'-Lumumba School.

Che'-Lumumba was a small non-traditional school housed in the Pan Africa Building at the University of Massachusetts, Amherst (UMASS). It was a small, resistance-fomenting elementary school (first to fifth grade) named after Che' Guevara and Patrice Lumumba. At any given time, there were approximately ten students at the school, which allowed for small class sizes and a tremendous amount of individualized attention.

16 *Feeling Race*

Our teachers were committed to changing the world. At school, we were taught Third World history, Black history, women's history, working-class history and critical thinking skills. We were purposefully taught OUR history and the history of OUR people so that we would have confidence in ourselves. At the same time, we were shown how to challenge authority in a respectful manner and ask questions about every single bit of information. We were taught to be fighters and challenge those with power. Our teachers and parents knew that this meant we would not be quiet or docile or accept the status quo. At Che'-Lumumba, we were exposed to the early stages of resistance work: organize, challenge, resist, fight back and rebuild.

My memories of growing up in Amherst are highly positive. Fighting racism, being immersed in a make-shift family created through organizing, having parties and being around people committed to social justice are inseparable to me. Even now – and at this point, I am 48 – memories flood back to the 1970s, and I can see my dad drinking Carl Rossi's red wine out of a round jug at the circular wooden kitchen table that my mom made in her "wood-working room" – while folks were meeting at our house. I remember my dad's voice as loud, and he would sometimes bang on the table with his fist or the palm of his hand saying, "I am in love with life and in love with the world; we must smash capitalism!"

These memories – of energy, of passion, of commitment, of being aware of myself as a child of color from the Third World – bring back very positive feelings. The beauty of Blackness and Brownness was demonstrated constantly by my parents, their friends and the community within which I lived. I was raised to feel good about myself as a person of color. Feeling race was an emotion full of pride and excitement, and it was a good and happy feeling.

Karnataka, India

Another vital component of my upbringing is that by the age of ten, my family and I lived in India three times. Living in India also shaped my racial consciousness.

My maternal grandmother was married to my maternal grandfather when she was 11. She had her first child at 13, the second one at 15 and my mother at 18, in 1940. By the time my mom was 18, she had graduated from college and was sent to live in Copenhagen, Denmark, where she lived for one year. She then went to Germany to live with her sister, who was a medical doctor who, at the time, worked in a German hospital.

My father was born in Queens (New York City) in 1943 to an unwed 17-year-old Italian girl. He was adopted as an infant by my grandparents, who were children of German immigrants. My father, an only child, was drafted into the Vietnam War in the late 1960s. He believed it was his duty to fight in the war, and his family agreed. He accepted his draft assignment, left New York and was sent to boot camp at 23. He proceeded to clerical school in Fort

Feeling Race 17

Jackson, South Carolina; was sent to San Antonio for Medical Records training; and, in August of 1967, arrived in Munich, Germany, where he served as a medical records specialist for the US Army.

When my mother arrived in Munich, Germany, in the 1960s, she got a job working as a medical clerk for the US Army at the same hospital where my dad was a medic. My mother, who was engaged to another man in a soon-to-be "arranged marriage," met my father while they were both clerking for the Army. They met at work when she was 26 and he was 23.

Soon after meeting my dad, my mother broke off her engagement, which shocked and upset her family. On February 8, 1968, my mom and dad were married. The wedding took place six months after they met. My parents wanted to get married outside under pine trees, but the Chaplain, who was angry about their impending inter-racial marriage (he had sent them to counseling because of this), refused their request and forced them to get married in the military chapel.

When my mother married my father in her peacock blue sari, it was just a few months after the 1967 Loving case overturned anti-miscegenation laws in the US, with the Supreme Court ruling such laws "unconstitutional." When my parents met in 1967, 17 southern states plus Oklahoma still enforced laws prohibiting inter-racial marriage between whites and "nonwhites."

My father was honorably discharged from the Army in 1968, and my parents moved to the USA. My mom arrived pregnant with me, her first child. I was born on June 11, 1969, in Amherst, Massachusetts.

In 1972, we moved to India for two years and lived there until 1974. My younger brother was born in India on July 19, 1973. When my brother was a little over a year old, we moved back to Amherst. In 1977 we moved back to India and lived there for 6–8 months. During that time period, I was "home-schooled." In 1980, we went back to India for a few months. When we returned, we moved to Wilmington, Delaware.

While living in India, we lived in multiple places. We lived in Dharwad, Karnataka State, while my dad taught English classes at Dharwad University. We also lived on and off with my mother's brother, who we affectionately referred to as "Dada," which means "Brother." We spent a lot of time living in Dada's house with his wife, three daughters and my maternal grandmother.

Remembering back 40 years is hard. Nonetheless, I do have feelings/memories about living in India. I usually wore a salwar kameez, a traditional Indian outfit with wide pants, which are narrow at the bottom, and a long flowing tunic. The tailor made me a green one with yellow and white flowers, which I loved, and I wore it all the time! I also remember taking bucket baths at night in a dimly lit bathroom with my cousins and then all of us running around the dark house lit by gas lamps in the evening. I remember being reminded to plug in the drain in the wall after our baths so cobras wouldn't slither into the house.

I remember going for walks with my parents that lasted entire days. They often walked to places where people were on strike, met with the workers about

18   *Feeling Race*

their demands and talked politics and revolution late into the night. I remember trekking through rice paddies and sugar cane fields on our way to meet people, and I remember being petrified that I was going to step on a cobra and get bitten. I remember eating freshly cut sugar cane and mangoes and guavas ripe off the tree. I remember the late-night meals, boisterous dinner talk and the passion in the conversations about workers' wages and working conditions. I remember us coming home late to my uncle's house and the fights he had with my parents about keeping dinner waiting while everyone wondered where we were. I remember wanting to live in India and not return to the US. I remember watching a lot of Hindi movies and wanting to be the beautiful Indian heroine with the bright sarees and the handsome husband. I remember brown and black skin, eating paan, and having coconut oil rubbed in my hair until I was a bright shining child. I remember flamboyant colors, blooming bougainvillea trees, radiant skin, white teeth, train rides and eating food with our fingers. I remember belonging and aching to belong permanently.

Stories are always complicated; my parents decided not to live in India in 1974. We moved back to Amherst, and in 1980, my parents decided to move to another state. They said they wanted to leave Amherst because they did not want to live in a "bubble." They wanted to live and raise their children in the "real" world.

Wilmington, Delaware

In 1978 we took a one-month cross-country trip from Massachusetts to Oregon. We drove our light blue Nissan station wagon in and out of cities and towns, across the Great Plains and into Arizona. We saw Salt Lake City, the snow-capped Rockies, went to the Pine Ridge Reservation in North Dakota and followed the heat into New Mexico. We played in fountains in Portland, Oregon, where we stayed with our friend Jill and her husband Ray, and then returned home. The trip was really a one-month-long field trip. We visited Harriet Tubman's grave, followed the Trail of Tears and experienced the ire of a racist baseball team in Utah. The trip was one more racial journey that shaped my life.

As we traveled across the country, my parents were looking for a place to live. At the time, I did not know this. They wanted out of Amherst. They wanted to move to New Mexico but decided against it because my paternal grandfather lived in New York. My father was an only child, so my parents wanted to remain close to him.

Ultimately, my parents decided to move to Wilmington, Delaware, because it was between NYC and DC and close to Baltimore. In the summer of 1980, we left Amherst. We did not know a single person in Delaware. My parents did not have jobs. One week they drove to Delaware and found a place to live, and then we packed up and moved. We NEVER returned to Amherst, not to visit, not to reconnect, not to remember. Our first return visit was on July 15, 2017, when I took my parents and my children to Amherst for the first time in 37 years.

Feeling Race 19

When we moved to Wilmington, Delaware, in the summer of 1980, we moved into an urban area wracked with racial tension. Five years before we moved to Wilmington, on the evening of August 17, 1975, Sheila Farrell, a 12-year-old Black girl, was shot to death by her white neighbor for "stealing" peaches from his backyard peach tree. John Bailey, the man who killed Sheila, shot her in her back and then chased her until she collapsed, unconscious, on her front porch. Telling the crowd of horrified bystanders that she had stolen "his furniture," Bailey then fled the scene (Bailey v. State 1976). The police were immediately called; the murderer was identified. Upon a search of the home, the police found Bailey hiding in his attic. He denied shooting Sheila. As the case progressed, protests, unrest and anger erupted throughout the city (Howell July 2020). At 11, I remember being horrified by what happened to Sheila. I remember fearing white people. I remember being afraid.

Although we did not live in Wilmington at the time of Sheila's murder, we moved into the area where Sheila was shot and killed. My parents talked about her and the "peach tree shooting" frequently. I remember walking to school – Warner Elementary – and I recall my mother telling me to stay out of "white people's yards" because, "remember, they shot Sheila." I recall feeling upset and sad about Sheila and angry at white people. How could they have killed a 12-year-old girl? A girl my age?

Another reason for the racial unrest was that Wilmington did not desegregate its public schools until 1978, and they did so only under a court-mandated order. The federal court order divided New Castle County (NCC) into four separate school districts. The city of Wilmington was divided into quadrants, and each of the four school districts was legally mandated to educate a portion of the "city" kids. Along with the new school districts came "forced" busing which resulted in angry whites protesting and organizing to challenge the constitutionality of court-mandated busing. Wilmington's desegregation plan required that city children (read "Black and Brown") be bused out of the city to suburban schools for nine years and suburban children (read "white") were bused into city schools for three years (Albright 2016).

It was within this context that we moved into Wilmington. And it was here that I came of age, learned there were strict racial lines and realized that Amherst was Dorothy's Kansas. When we moved to Wilmington, Delaware, race was real and sharp, and people lived in neighborhoods based on race. Segregation was new to me. There were few families that were "mixed," and people seemed unaware of India and Indians. Everyone thought we were Puerto Rican or that we were just light-skinned. It was in Wilmington that I grew ashamed of my Indian heritage.

When we moved to Wilmington, we moved into a predominantly Black, working-class neighborhood. We moved into the Ninth Ward, now known as the "North Side," and were apparently the first "Puerto Ricans" to move onto the block. This was funny to us because we were not Puerto Rican! Kids

20 *Feeling Race*

often asked why we did not move to Fourth Street (the Spanish section of Wilmington). Even when I told people we weren't Spanish, most people did not believe me. Kids would refer to me as a Puerto Rican, and when I would say I wasn't, they'd ask if I was Black or white, Black or white, Black or white? In Wilmington, there were clear racial demarcations which I was forced to learn.

My mother, who was beautiful, fun, loud and engaging, now became an embarrassment to me and my brother when she showed up in a sari or salwar kameez. And when she wore a bindi, both my brother and I often refused to go with her. It was in Wilmington that I learned we did not fit into the racial schemata.

As a teenager, I vividly recall a conversation I had with our neighbor "Grace." Grace lived next door, on the second floor. One day she was talking to me, and she referred to me as Black. I responded that I wasn't Black, and she yelled at me. She told me to stop lying and pretending my dad was white. "We all know he's light-skinned, but he's still Black, no matter how hard you act as if he is not," she said as she walked down her front porch steps that sunny afternoon.

Trying to fit my "Third World" self into a strict racial order was hard and painful. I was constantly bombarded with questions about my race. Since I was raised to identify as a woman of color, and the only women of color in my neighborhood were Black women and girls, I quickly placed myself firmly in the Black/Brown space. Once the kids in my neighborhood and in school saw which side I had chosen, both literally and figuratively (if you also considered our neighborhood) – I was taken to be a mixed child or a light-skinned Black girl.

Growing up, I remember being called glow-worm, light-bright, Puerto Rican, red-bone, high yella, light-skinned, mulatto, Spanish, half and half, etc. Sometimes the names were meant as compliments, and, sometimes, they were thrown as insults. Constantly being asked, "What are you?" was discombobulating and always left me feeling like an outsider. In Amherst, I fit into the racial schemata, but in Wilmington, I had to choose "Black" or "white" – and neither identity fully captured me or how I felt on the inside.

Wilmington was very different from Amherst. In our new neighborhood, people were looking for jobs, working night shifts and trying to keep their children from police violence, teen pregnancy, drugs and being shot. This space was very different from Amherst. In Wilmington, my parents' friends worked long hours, and here, in this urban space, Blackness and Brownness marked you for profiling and discrimination in real and hard ways.

University of Delaware

In June 1987, I walked across the John Dickinson High School football field stage to receive my high school diploma. My boyfriend, who was out on bail for an arrest for shooting someone in the foot over a drug deal gone bad, was there. Later that summer, we "broke up" when he was convicted as a minor and

Feeling Race 21

sent to an adult prison, and I went off to college to work on my BA in Sociology with a minor in Black American Studies at the University of Delaware (UD), in Newark, Delaware.

My first year on campus, I commuted. Newark, Delaware, was a 30-minute ride by car from my house in Wilmington. However, I rode the bus to get to school, and that took over an hour. I felt out of place at the University of Delaware, a Primarily White Institution (PWI). In Amherst, I lived and went to school primarily with people of color; in India, my father was the only white person I saw for years; and when we moved to Wilmington, I lived in a predominantly African American neighborhood. At UD, however, I was often the only person of color in white spaces. I felt uncomfortable amid so much whiteness because, to me, whiteness was synonymous with violence and terrorism.

The majority of white America, I knew – from books, from Che'-Lumumba and from my lived experiences – refused to stand with people of color. They were the oppressors and engaged in – and supported – state-sanctioned violence against us. At a young age, I was exposed to the history of the Americas, Africa and India, and I was aware of the genocide, murder and torture whites systematically inflicted on people of color.

As such, whites who were not part of the anti-racist movement or who were not explicitly talking about and fighting against racism made me uneasy. At UD, I was aware of a new environment, and I knew that I had to be careful. Here I was often the only person of color in a classroom, or in a line, or in the dining hall or walking to my class. I had to adjust to a new way of being and living. The ease of being outspoken faded away. I became scared. The fear rooted in me deep down, causing me to be vigilant in the attempt to keep myself safe. At UD, I experienced a new type of check-your-reality fear because here, white students and professors often said racist things, and I knew that racism spoken led to racism enacted.

Example #1: In 1990, I pledged Delta Sigma Theta Sorority, Inc. at the University of Delaware. One warm spring afternoon in early April, when we were "on line" (actively pledging), we walked through campus, passing Mitchell Hall. There were a lot of students outside, it was starting to get dark, and we were headed to the food hall. I remember that late afternoon vividly, although I am thinking back to 30+ years ago. A white male student saw us, called us "Niggers" from his third-floor window, and then continued to yell racial slurs at us. I remember being startled and upset. This memory is still sharp and painful, decades later, here and now. I remember the word "Nigger" echoing in the quad and other white students looking and laughing in the twilight.

Example #2: I took a winter session class when I was a junior. I honestly cannot even remember the name of the class. I do, however, remember that the class was taught by a young white female who was a graduate student working on her PhD in sociology or history. I also believe she said her dad taught at UD. During one of her lectures, she was talking about Harlem and Jazz, and she made a comment and then added, "back when Harlem was civilized."

22 *Feeling Race*

I remember the classroom: it was big and we were in an old building. We met in the afternoon, and the room was dark and warm and my body felt languid. I just wanted to chill out and get something to eat after class. Once she made her remark, however, the slowness, ease and comfort of the warm room left my body. With the utterance of those words, I was immediately hyper-alert, angry and I was, once again, the only person of color in the room. My body became rigid. I didn't want to say anything. I did not want to challenge authority; I did not want to be the only person in the room who was offended; I did not want to speak up and be the one person to disrupt the easiness of the winter afternoon. However, I felt like my body and my integrity were on the line. I felt it was my duty to speak up and not let this remark or this woman slide off the hook. Silence was not an option in this space, although I longed for it to be. I remember feeling like I was watching my body from across the room in slow motion. I looked around the room. No one seemed bothered by her comment. Some students even laughed. I remember raising my hand, although that was the LAST thing I wanted to do that day. I remember asking her what she said. "Can you please repeat your last remark?" I asked. She did. I asked her what she meant. I remember her adding to her response that Harlem was civilized in the past but that today it was overrun with addicts and the homeless. I remember telling her that her words were racist. Her face flushed; I could see the red in the darkened room. She apologized defensively, but the damage was done. I left, fast and hurried, harried and alone. My hands were shaking, and my heart was pounding.

Fear made me WANT to be quiet and slip unnoticed from scary white places. Fear had a vice grip around my throat, paralyzing me, hurting me. However, since I was often the "only one" in my classes, I felt like I HAD to speak out. If I didn't, I felt weak, muzzled, powerless. The relationship between speaking out and silence was (and is) complicated for me. It was (and is) a terrain filled with fear and ambivalence, as well as the obligatory duty to constantly resist and challenge oppression.

At UD, I was outnumbered by whites and white ideas, and I became nervous speaking out. I was often intimidated by my white peers in the classroom because I knew that, as a group, whites would band together (against me). I felt like I was up against a mob every time I opened my mouth to speak, and thus, I longed to be silent. Simultaneously, however, I also felt that I was obligated to speak out and challenge the racist and classist ideas circulating in my classrooms. I struggled to give birth to my voice while suffocating in a culture of whiteness. When I did allow myself to speak, I trembled. I was scared, alone and unsupported. In this space, I became afraid.

Cecil County Community College

After I graduated from UD with my BA in Sociology in 1991, I worked for a year at Cecil County Community College (CCCC) in Elkton, Maryland. The job was funded by a grant designed to get women on welfare to return to college. In the early 1990s, Elkton was primarily white, small and poor. Part of my job required me to go to women's houses – which were usually located in mobile parks – and talk to them. The women were often unfriendly and gave me the cold shoulder. I wondered why they were so rude.

After about two weeks on the job, my supervisor told me I could not go on anymore "home visits" and that she wanted me to leave at 4 PM every day. I protested and told her I needed to work until 5 PM to get my full pay. She said she was sending me home at 4 because winter was approaching, it was getting dark earlier, and she did not want me in Elkton after dark. "This is Klan country," she said. She told me she could not take it if I was beaten up, hurt or killed. She said I could not go on anymore "home visits" because she honestly thought I might get physically hurt – "beat up or worse." She said, "They don't like Blacks here." She told me I would receive my full check but that she wanted me to be safe. I was learning to always be afraid of whiteness – and this second academic experience made me realize that education is a safe space for some groups but not us.

The University of Maryland, Baltimore County

After I worked in Cecil County for a year, I went to the University of Maryland, Baltimore County (UMBC) to earn an MA in Applied Sociology (1991–1994). At UMBC, I was awarded a Teaching Assistantship (TA). My first year at the school, I did not have to teach, but in my second year, I was asked to give one or two Introduction to Sociology lectures for the professor for whom I was a TA. I literally could not do it. I begged him to let me do more grading, provide more tutorial support, meet with students more frequently and literally do anything else besides teach. He was compassionate and did not force me to lecture, and for that, I will be eternally grateful. I was so scared of teaching that I truly felt like I would lose my voice if I had to give a presentation. In learning to be afraid, I lost faith in myself.

At UMBC, I was scared to talk in class – and by now, I was scared to talk, period, not only about race but about anything, in public places. While I was working on my MA, I had to do an oral presentation for my methodology class with Dr. Adler. During the oral presentation on healthcare, my voice shook so much that she stopped me in the middle and asked me to come with her in the hallway. Once outside, she put her arm around me and asked if something bad had happened to me and if I was going to cry. She was clearly very concerned with my state of being and even said that if I did not want to finish the presentation, I did not have to do so. I remember saying I would finish, and I did, and I recollect the other students cheering me on when I finished. I was horrified by the entire ordeal.

By this point in my life, I experienced a lot of time feeling threatened by whites in the classroom and out in the community. I felt browbeaten, constantly

24 *Feeling Race*

dreading the next racist remark, knowing I would have to respond and that I would often have no support from others because I would, once again, be the only Brown person in white spaces. I ended up scared, alienated, alone and feeling under attack. Even though my early experiences and education had mired revolutionary theory in my body and brain, my confidence was shaken, and I did not know how to regain it.

Conclusion

I have always felt race. At first, I felt race deeply, in a self-affirming, jarringly beautiful and powerful way. I have always loved Blackness and Brownness and associate it with strength, passion, activism and love. The positive feelings I had of being a Brown girl, however, twisted when we moved to Wilmington, Delaware. Race for me, at that time, morphed into actively realizing that: (1) white people did not want you in their spaces, especially in their schools and neighborhoods, (2) racist whites could and would hurt you, either in the classroom by destroying your confidence or out on the streets by profiling you and harassing you, (3) America created whiteness which was centered and then there were the "others," (4) outside of our bubble of Amherst, a college town, American society did not recognize multiculturalism or bi-raciality – one was either white or Black, there was no middle ground, and (5) one had to choose a racial side at an early age.

As I grew into a teenager and young adult, this understanding of racism hurt, confused and angered me. Race is a rip current through my life – I learned early that Blackness and Brownness are magnificent and irresistible and that race is also a "thing" used to terrorize, humiliate and destroy people. I believe my experiences growing up in mixed race environment which focused on Black and Brown power in the 1970s, my life and travels to India and immersion in (our) multicultural and multi-ethnic households, and my harsh "coming of age" and "coming to racism" experiences in Delaware and Maryland caused me to feel race in every cell of my being at all times. I always feel race.

Donna-Marie

The Move to the Suburbs

In my dreams, I hunted for a place to hide.
Harriet Tubman, Underground Railroad, a bridge
to the other side.

Born to another place. Born to another time.
Running away a ten-year-old,
to the house of someone kind.

Feeling Race 25

Davy Crockett scavenger hunts, bottle caps, faded pennies,
 unlit matches.
Wavering flames, firemen, black snake firehose,
A match lit, the backyard garbage can in ashes.

Daddy home early,
stripping off his belt,
"I'm going to give you a whipping," he barked,
"The kind you've never felt!"

Red Ked sneakers dashed to freedom.
Brown Body trembling, refusing to be hit.
Rabid gorilla daddy trailing me,
foaming at the bit.

"You think you'll get a whipping, and everything will be fine.
We're moving to the suburbs; You've run away for the last time."

"I ain't gonna run away from home no more,"
I pleaded.
I ain't going to run away from home no more," I cried.
"They speak English correctly in the suburbs," was his only reply.

Figure 1.2 Donna-Marie at an African history museum in Senegal, West Africa

26   *Feeling Race*

Facing fire fascinated me. I sat in wonderment my first time in front of a blazing campfire in my Mickey Mouse t-shirt, singing folk songs with the hippie camp counselors, who, for me, at the age of eight, were my mothers away from home. When I came home from camp, I began collecting used books of matches in my Davy Crockett scavenger hunts in the park across the street. Soon afterward, from the window of my bedroom, I could see my parents watching two firemen with a long hose extinguishing a small fire in the garbage can in our backyard. With the sudden realization that the match that I had blown-out and thrown away had somehow reignited itself, I fled from the house in fear of my father's wrath. There was no time to pack a suitcase.

Six short months after running away from home, my older brother, younger sister and I were packed into our station wagon, transported up a mountain, past a subdivision with newly built homes across from deteriorating farmhouses, down streets that were called roads to our new home in a Connecticut suburb: 328 Huckleberry Hill Road. A suburban town, where as my grandmother put it, "other race people" lived. Back then, the "salt of the earth" working class of old Yankee stock sold the farmland of their ancestors to the growing numbers of white upper-middle classes leaving the city to graze in greener pastures. Ambitious land developers were turning Avon's untouched wooded acreage into subdivisions with freshly watered, well-maintained, manicured yards and well-ordered flower beds. They built colonial style five- bedroom cookie cutter homes turning dirt roads into well-paved private streets with dead-end cul-de-sacs. We lived in a well-preserved wooded area and humorously called our long pebbled driveway "Watermelon Lane" because, at the time, it was still thought that "Blacks love themselves some watermelon."

To School and Back

Long pebbled driveway. Glass covered home.
I thought of the boy I once knew, scar running down his cheek.

Waiting for a big yellow school bus. Waiting for it alone.
Onto a school bus I climbed that day. No one at my side.
Into a sea of milk-white faces I walked. There was no place to hide.

Running away from home I dreamed,
Past giggles and whispers suspended.

Hot lava flushing my face,
I ran up a hill that never ended.
Hunting in my picture drawer for a face that could not be miserable,
I packed a negro girl in a brown paper bag that day.
I buried her invisible.

Feeling Race   27

I was the only negro girl in the classroom. I never knew, from one day to the next, what surprises awaited me. I tried to make myself invisible from the back of the bus to the back of the classroom, but I wasn't Houdini.

Coming home on the school bus on three different days, I looked out the window to witness a circle of fire burning on my front lawn. Watching a fire burning in a perfect man-made circle instilled in me a fear of fire that would remain with me my entire life. The first selectman of the town had informed my father that it would be in his best interest to let his group purchase our home so as not to disrupt the status quo. The fire was certainly people's warning to my father that his stubborn refusal not to budge might have repercussions.

"In the South, the Klan burned black men and tied them to the cross of Jesus," my father cautioned me one evening with a family history narrative about his father's favorite uncle. As a young boy, my father's favorite uncle, a self-educated lawyer, had been killed getting out the Black vote in the small town where they lived in Ashdown, Arkansas. "Don't worry," my father said reassuringly, "We're not in Arkansas!" It took some time before I could sleep through the night without waking-up in the early morning hours to see if there was the smell of smoke in the air.

"I must be perfect, a good little Black girl, a credit to my race," I told myself, counting the red welts across my brown body, week after week. Not sparing the rod was a form of social control the formerly enslaved learned from the slave master to use on their progeny with impunity. Although the scars have healed, they have never gone away. Tuberculosis had ravaged my mother's lungs, and this was the reason we moved to the fresh air of the countryside. This move inadvertently thrust us into the boiling center of the Civil Rights movement and the fight for residential integration in the north. As children, we are promised a time of innocence. As a child soldier inducted by circumstance into the movement for equality and social justice, this move cost me mine.

The Playground

In my city neighborhood, I was King of the Hill, Queen of the Nile. I had earned my place of respect on the playground. At the beginning of recess, we selected sides singing in a circle around a girl in the middle. Each girl had her turn to be in the middle of the circle – eyes closed, one arm stretched out, aiming toward the girls in the circle. She slowly spins around in a circle like the hands of a clock as everyone sings sassily:

Little Sally Walker sitt'n in a saucer,
Rise Sally rise, wipe your weep'n eyes.
Put your hands on your hips,
Let your backbone slip.
You can shake it to the east, Sally,

28   *Feeling Race*

You can shake it to the west, Sally.
You can shake it to the very one
That you love the best!

The girls run out the door for recess. It was the first time someone suggested, "Let's play volleyball." We all run toward the girl's space in the school yard – a space closest to the school building. Anxious to start, each girl takes a place in line to be selected for the winning side. Rushing past the girls, Susie, the alpha girl and aspiring teacher in the class, takes a position at the front of the line and turns around to face everyone. She then proceeds to go down the human chain, pointing to one eager body and then the next, singsongingly reciting:

"Eenie, meenie, miney, mo, catch a nigger by the toe" Before she could continue, I instinctively reacted, popping Susie in the head, leaving her unhurt but surprised and confused.

"You're calling me a nigger!" I shouted.
"No, I'm not!" she responded, rubbing her head in disbelief.
"Yes, you are!"
"No, I'm not!"
"Then, who's the nigger?"
"What's a nigger? It's just a song."
"Well, go home and look up the word, stupid; it's in the dictionary."

Third Grade Classroom

All heads turned in my direction as Miss Smith described to the class how dark-skinned Africans, before coming to America, would swing from tree to tree like Tarzan and Jane. Teachers are so knowledgeable, I thought at that age. I didn't dare tell my third-grade teacher to go home and look up evolution in the encyclopedia that I knew sat on her bookshelf as it did on mine. Still, I did go home that day to look in the mirror for where my tail had been cut off.

Middle School

Moving between childhood and adulthood, my middle school ritual began with tucking blond Barbie into the bottom of my book bag, then up sweeping my Annette Funicello flip, painting white frosted lipstick across my lips (that matched my same color nail polish) before leaving the house gingerly, so as not to catch a run in my stockings as I rushed to catch the school bus. I had assimilated into the world that had been thrust upon me. My sense of race and identity was in a state of flux.

"That's it. Like it or not, I'm sending you to private school," my authoritative father barked, coming through the front door directly from a seventh grade

Feeling Race   29

parent-teacher conference. The fact that the teacher said I was doing well, with a report card full of Cs and Ds, had him in a state of rage – both at me for not studying and at racism within the suburban public school system that wanted me to fail academically.

Convinced that his daughter would soon be placed on the non-college track to become a below-low-wage worker at McDonald's, my father, a graduate of Monroe Colored High School in the South, yanked me out of my comfortable public school environment and threw me into the unknown waters of private education. He was a product of the segregated South and separate but unequal schooling and was determined that his children would receive the kind of quality education that he could only dream of.

Seventh Grade Private School

Manicured lawns, a stately stone-built mansion and rolling hills as far as the eyes could roam, boys and girls spilled out of wood-lined station wagons, carrying white canvas book bags and girls wearing funny brown shoes with a flap in the front, called brogues. It was down South in Birmingham, Alabama, that four little girls died attending Sunday school in the basement of their church. Rosa Parks refused to give up her seat in the front of the bus. George Wallace blocked the entrance of his state university from colored boys and girls. And here I was, integrating another all-white school. This one was more exclusive than the last. But where were the flashing cameras and barking police dogs and why wasn't the governor at the door? The door that I would suffer behind for three years!

As the headmistress delivered a back-to-school assembly address to her flock of young minds on the responsibilities of class in a voice slightly above a whisper, I looked around at my newly designated classmates and sank into the quicksand of freshly scrubbed faces, jackets and ties, skirts that matched sweaters and knee socks and braces wrapped around perfect teeth as everyone stood up to sing "God Bless America."

"Mr. K. is the coolest teacher in the upper school," my new classmates informed me. He was against the war in Vietnam and looked like the painting of Jesus Christ in the stained-glass windows of my church. No one believed that Mr. K. could possibly be what I happened to see in him: a bigot behind peace and flower power.

Mrs. T. wasn't the Hunchback of Notre Dame, but I imagined she looked like him, especially since she was bent over and had a few hairs on her chin that masculinized her. She proudly instilled the fear of God in her students, each vying to favorably impress her since she had such high, unable-to-reach standards of academic excellence. Seated on her imperial throne, Her Highness of the English department demanded that her minions greatly respect the classics of Western literature – books way beyond our comprehension. Since my

30 *Feeling Race*

first day in school, Mrs. T. refused to look at me. I had it all figured out. She ignored me because I was too dumb to be worth teaching. Better to be ignored than dead, I thought to myself as my shadow walked out the door onto the field hockey playing field, where I ran faster and hit the ball harder than any of the girls in my school.

Only the latest Nancy Drew mystery on the shelf of the public library or the latest Newsweek Magazine on our living room coffee table could entice me to read a story from beginning to end. But I was determined to change Mrs. T.'s understanding of me. I decided to read one of her favorite books, though not in the canon of great literature, *The Wind in the Willows* (1961). I didn't expect to like it very much. I didn't expect to find characters that made me laugh until my ribcage hurt. I didn't expect to find characters that I understood and could see my world through. But I did. Over and over again, I regaled myself with the author's description of a tiny little conceited frog, dashingly elegant and dapperly dressed in a tuxedo, looking at himself in the mirror and imagining himself a swashbuckling hero as he sings a song about his exaggerated exploits to his enraptured audience of vacant chairs.

I laughed and laughed, delighted with the character of Mr. Frog of Frog Hollow, the narcissist. I decided to include a personally designed invitation to Mr. Frog of Frog Hollow's elegant dinner party, which was my favorite chapter in the book. I slowly wrote, almost to exhaustion, a hand-written invitation. Folded in half, sheets of white paper were tossed into the trash until I was finally satisfied with my fancy calligraphy.

I placed the invitation with the illustration under my book report and handed them to Mrs. T. as I left class that day. I imagined a smile invading Mrs. T.'s face as she read the invitation – her humped back straightening from laughter evoked from reading the pretentiousness and utter pomposity in the words that I had chosen to invite her to fictitious Mr. Frog's elegant dinner party.

No Response to the Invitation. Book Report: C

Winter homes for skiing, summer vacations in Europe, maids with Irish accents, race and class would not leave my mind. Being the only one in the room made me feel different from everyone else in the room. For a day, I visited an inner-city school filled with low-income black students my age. Even in this classroom setting, I was made to feel different. This teacher, a friend of the family who brought me there, made a point of my class difference to her inquisitive students. I was show and tell for the day. "This is Donna. She doesn't live in the city. She lives in the suburbs. She goes to school with white boys and girls." I could feel their gaze poking and prodding my entire body, searching for difference. There was no safe haven for me. In every classroom, I had become the only one in the room.

The world was changing, but school remained the same. Mrs. T.'s humiliating C grade continued to haunt me. I identified with Beaver Cleaver on TV, constantly ruminating about being different from everyone else. "I think I'll wear a peace sign around my neck and tie a rawhide string around it," I said to myself. Peace rallies, civil rights protests, upper-class boys didn't go to war, and if they enlisted didn't see combat. Black, Brown and working-class white boys were called men. They went to war, and their sisters worried that they would not be coming home. In English class, I returned to my vivid daydreams like the ones I had in other classes. I yearned to be lying in bed with a good Newsweek magazine and the latest Nancy Drew mystery.

Mary

As a young child, I learned about race primarily through my grandma's behavior around Black people in Rogers Park, a Chicago neighborhood that was undergoing significant racial change. I describe this racial socialization as learning to be quietly color-conscious, a color consciousness steeped in the fear of blackness. It was in fourth grade that I began to make sense of this socialization through the bold decision of my teacher to implement the "blue eyes/brown eyes" exercise, created by anti-racist educator Jane Elliott the day after Martin Luther King was assassinated. My participation in this exercise was racially transformative for my young self, causing me to seriously reflect on my learned anti-Blackness. Yet it wasn't until my early teenage years that I began to understand that my family's anti-Blackness was a part of the racial

Figure 1.3 Mary and brother Jim with Grandpa Joe, Circa 1978

32 *Feeling Race*

problem that Miss Martin so fearlessly outlined, and not until my twenties that I realized that I, myself, was implicated in this oppression. It was at this same time, in the early 1990s, that I was beginning to understand not only my connection to the rioting in the streets, in the music and in the movies but in my connection to the larger system of white supremacy, and in my own agency to challenge such a system.

Waking Up to Silence

My grandma always moved at a hurried pace. Whether we were on our way to church, to get jelly bismarck donuts for breakfast or to the *Jewel* for that night's supper, grandma was on the move. I cannot remember ever lingering on the sidewalk or browsing in a store with my grandma; she was always on a mission. My grandma moved her mouth at an equally hurried pace. She wasn't a grandma who dished out sage advice or life lessons; she was simply a "chit chatter." She talked about the weather, about what we would have for dinner, about what games we would play when we got back to her house, and of course, about her beloved Chicago Cubs. I don't remember grandma talking about anything serious. Her seriousness only became apparent in her silences, and it was in her silences that I learned about race. Grandma's chatter kept up with her footsteps as we rushed to the bakery before it closed, but then suddenly, grandma would stop talking, grab my hand tightly and pull me quickly across the street. And then the chatter would continue. It didn't take long for me to notice the pattern: Black Person – Silence – Fear – Avoidance. Nobody ever explained this to me, but I felt the fear in my grandma's grip on my hand and understood that we were going out of our way to avoid the threat coming toward us. No words were needed. And then in 1977, when I was about ten years old, the silence was broken by my fourth grade teacher, Miss Martin.

It started one morning in our classroom portable when Miss Martin informed us that some changes were going to be made and that she needed to divide the class by eye color. Those with brown eyes, she explained, were deserving of some privileges from which the blue-eyed students would need to be excluded. I shared some nervous laughter with my blue-eyed peers as Miss Martin directed us to a back corner of the room in an uncharacteristically gruff manner. My nervous feelings quickly became feelings of outrage as the brown-eyed kids waltzed off to their exclusive recess, and the outrage slowly turned to sadness and disbelief that Miss Martin, warm and generous Miss Martin, was treating us in this way. On the second day of the exercise, when the blue eyes were the privileged group, I didn't just feel it; I *got* it. I really understood what she was trying to teach us. I could barely hold back my tears when she told one of the brown-eyed kids that he was too messy to be trusted with the paints because brown-eyed kids were careless. My mind flashed to those walks with grandma, and I began to feel not just my grandma's fear but to feel the victims of her fear. *How must they feel*, I asked myself, *when we rush across the street?*

Feeling Race   33

And it was then that I could imagine what they might be feeling: nervousness, outrage, sadness and disbelief. Miss Martin woke me up.

That same year, the miniseries *Roots* came out. I watched all of it, as did my family, but we didn't talk about it. Levar Burton's back and his tears were both difficult and awe-inspiring to watch. The white violence and hostility were both horrifying and devastating to watch. The next year, *The White Shadow* premiered, a TV series about a white basketball coach in a "tough" urban high school. I loved this show. I fell in love with star players Coolidge, Hayward and Gomez. I wanted them to succeed, and I wanted *Coach* to help them do so. And so he did. Coach stepped in again and again to *save* his athletes from a myriad of problems they had with teachers, girls, gangs and alcohol – Coach was always there. This was the kind of white people I wanted my white people, my white family, to be. But this was not to be.

How it Felt to be a Problem

I visited my Florida grandparents once by myself as an adolescent. This was a huge treat. This meant Disney World, Sea World, chameleons, fresh orange juice and trips to "the club." Riding in the back of their big car driving to the "club" where I could swim and eat all day, we drove up a long, dusty road lined with older Black people selling fruits and vegetables. Coming from Chicago, I had never seen roadside markets like these. I was curious. I waited for my grandparents to explain or to perhaps stop the car so we could explore or buy something, just as they had done with the other curious things we drove past in what felt like a foreign land to me. But my grandparents didn't stop. They didn't even acknowledge the Black faces we passed. I took their cue and never asked. Their silence made me feel uncomfortable, but at this point, it was not unexpected. But the silence didn't last.

Grandpa Joe always sat in the lazy boy chair in the Florida sunroom to watch his programs. Usually, he offered a sweet compliment to me, that I "was getting all grown up" or that I "looked beautiful" when I walked past the television on my way outside to pick oranges from the tree or to play croquet. But on one pass-through, there was no compliment. Instead, grandpa Joe screamed the N-word and threw the candy bowl toward his program. I kept walking. But I was a little frightened. Grandpa Joe, who called me his "little darling," behaved like a raving lunatic because a Black person, a newscaster, was telling him about something he didn't want to hear. Were my white people the ones Miss Martin warned us about? Were my white people the ones who tortured Levar Burton? I didn't have a clear answer in my head yet. But I really wanted one.

After I returned home from my Florida visit, I wrote to my Florida grandma, asking for her advice, explaining to her that I had a Black friend and that other kids were being mean to us. This story was completely untrue because there *were no* Black kids in my class or in my neighborhood. Grandma wrote back,

34 *Feeling Race*

telling me not to let the other kids bother me. I felt relieved that my grandma didn't tell me to dump my imaginary Black friend, but I also felt very confused. What kind of white people *were* we? I didn't want to be associated with the white people that hurt Black people the way Miss Martin did in her lesson, but that tight grip and that candy bowl were making it hard for me to run away. How did it feel to be a problem? It felt really bad. But that feeling dissipated as I entered my teens. I didn't have time to feel bad because I was too busy feeling myself, my boyfriend and the freedom that came with my entry into young adulthood.

When I got to college in 1985, I met my two roommates – Jeanie, a Black girl who had Luther Vandross on endless repeat when she was blue and Starpoint's *Object of My Desire* when she was ready to party, and Marie, a white girl with a serious devotion to the "hair metal" bands of the 1980s: Motley Crue, Guns N' Roses and of course, Bon Jovi. Jeanie and I sang *Object of My Desire* at the top of our lungs, sometimes more than three times in a row, most days of the week. It was just that kind of a song. Jeanie was one of two African American girls on our dormitory floor. The other girl left before the first semester ended because she was pregnant. Jeanie didn't live far from campus and was spending less and less time in the dorm as time went by, and when she was in the dorm, Luther was playing. I remember walking in the room one day, and she was standing in front of our little TV watching *The Jeffersons*. She looked sad and/or bored. To lighten the mood, I came up behind her and squeezed her shoulders, and "joked" something along the lines of, "What are you watching that N- stuff for?" Yes, gasp. I can't explain it. It haunts me still. I loved *The Jeffersons*. And I loved Jeanie. Jeanie made it through the year but didn't come back after that. It really wasn't until *after* I graduated college in 1989 that I began to realize that *I* was, indeed, the problem.

A Second Awakening: How it Felt to Address the Problem

1989 was the year *Do The Right Thing* came out, and along with it, Public Enemy's *Fear of a Black Planet* and wow, I was just blown away as some of my questions from my adolescence started to be answered. With Danny Aiello's *Do The Right Thing* character, Sal, I was learning how "good" white people could also be racist and hence, that *my* white people, and even *I*, could be racist. It didn't feel good to see myself or my family in this way, but it really was revelatory because, ironically, it clarified for me that race was confusing. The ending of the movie, when the police choke Radio Raheem to death, also clarified for me that while white people, my people, were the problem, white cops were the biggest problem of all. Then, in 1992 came the Rodney King verdict. Having watched the cops beat King so severely and so clearly again and again and again, this not-guilty verdict was shocking to me. I was at a white friend's house in Seattle when the verdict was announced on the news. We were drinking, and I began screaming obscenities. My emotions were overflowing. I felt

Feeling Race 35

anger, outrage and the desire for revenge and said as much. My friend was also upset, but it wasn't the same. "Yeah, let's take this shit down!" she hollered but then collapsed on the couch with laughter. She wasn't serious. I was. I didn't want to be a part of the problem anymore. I didn't allow myself to feel sorry for Reginald Denny, the white truck driver who was dragged out of his truck and beaten while L.A. burned in the aftermath of the verdict. Instead, I turned up PE's *Fight The Power* louder. I began reading a lot. I read Malcolm, I read Baldwin, I read Angela Davis and I read histories of the Civil Rights Movement. I was a white girl in Seattle wearing a "By Any Means Necessary" shirt, daring my white family and friends to challenge me and my newfound knowledge. I felt anger and impatience with white people, white society and *my* white people, who were racially asleep or indifferent, or worse. And this new racially conscious identity was what I brought with me to Temple's graduate sociology program in 1994. I didn't hold a color-consciousness steeped in fear and anger towards Blackness but a consciousness steeped in a real animosity towards whiteness. No, I didn't hate myself, but I hated what I was a part of. I knew nothing, really – nothing about sociology, but after scouring course catalogs looking for classes about race, sociology seemed to be my only hope. And when I audited Howie Winant's race class, where the first book we read was his *Racial Formation in the United States*, I knew I was where I needed to be. At first, I just couldn't believe that other white people wanted to talk critically (I learned to use this word in grad school) about whiteness and white supremacy. I didn't have any white friends at that point who had much interest in really talking about race with me. I had a few who would listen to me, and I had two Black friends who would talk with me but would also tire of me – I hadn't realized then that Black people might NOT want to talk all the time about white supremacy with their white friends – or their Black ones.

So finding myself in a class devoted to talking about race was really, as cliché as it sounds, a dream come true. I had so many questions and such a sense of urgency. When I began really learning about theories of race and understanding how institutional discrimination worked, I was really taken aback. I couldn't believe this had all been kept from me! Knowing that white supremacy didn't just "happen" but was intentionally and strategically constructed out of pure political and economic greed gave me the truths I needed to solve *my* problem, to *resist* the system. I was ready to enter the classroom and share these truths. It felt good.

Michelle

The Breath of the Sixties: The Power of Civil Rights

I am literally a product of the 1960s and the opportunities that were created for Black Americans (Americans of African descent) by Civil Rights legislation. I was born three years after the Brown v. Board of Education decisions. My

36 Feeling Race

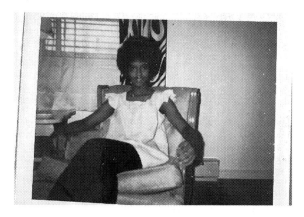

Figure 1.4 The breath of the Civil Rights Era and the sound of Black power
Source: Photographer unknown

story is not about being bussed and the object of integration into white spaces. It is instead one of empowerment, consciousness and certainty in myself and my Blackness. My feeling of race, my race, begins with a simple awareness of myself and my safety in the relationships of my family, the protection of my mother, the hot summer sun and the friendships of my neighborhood. In these relationships and the energy of the time – Black consciousness, Black rights, Black power, Black beauty – I was molded into the woman that I became. Certain of myself, my beauty and the stride of my walk, I stepped into the opportunities of the Civil Rights era with an empowered consciousness.

One of my earliest memories is a conversation between me and my brother Ronald. I know that I was not yet five because Miss Pat, the lady who lived in the apartment below us (there were three, one on the first floor, Miss Pat's on the second floor and ours on the third floor), took care of me while my mother was at work. Ronald was a teenager, he lived at his father's house, but he visited us often. He was walking past the bathroom door. I had left it open. He stopped to tell me to close the door when I am in the bathroom. Before he got it closed, I asked, "What are these for?" I was pointing to my eyes. He looked at me as if I were crazy and said, "To see with," and he closed the door.

Television has a large place in what I remember from my pre-five days and my life in that apartment. Everything was broadcast in black and white. I don't remember the times that TV came on and went off the air, but I remember the image that was on the screen when nothing was being broadcast. My brother Stephen and I watched everything together. He is two years older than me. Our absolute favorite show was Mr. Ed the talking horse. I can still remember the theme song. I think that it was bedtime when Mr. Ed ended. In the morning, we watched a kid's show hosted by Mr. Greenjeans that featured cartoons: Daffy

Feeling Race 37

Duck, Bugs Bunny, Elmore Fudd and our all-time favorite, Popeye the Sailor Man. We liked all of the characters: Olive Oyl, Popeye's girlfriend; Sweet Pea, a baby that Wikipedia says arrived in Popeye's mail; Bluto, the villain that skinny Popeye could beat once he had eaten spinach; and Wimpy, who would kindly pay you tomorrow for a hamburger today.

The other television event that still stands out in my mind is the airing of *Porgy and Bess*. According to Wikipedia, it aired on television once in 1967. I was ten, and I remember my mother talking about it, and I watched at least some of it. Its significance for me is not about the story itself but the demonstration of skin color, feminine beauty and masculinity. You see, my mother was light-skinned like Dorothy Dandridge and Lena Horne. Her hair was straight, her features were fine and her body petite. My father was tall, about 6'3; he had a big barrel chest, muscles and rich deep brown skin. I am my father's color with my mother's features, except my hair. It is soft, as opposed to hard, but its natural texture is nappy, not straight. My mother took meticulous care of my hair. As pointed out to me by my daughters, in all of the photographs from my childhood, my hair is shoulder length and straightened.

I never questioned my beauty. My family in general and my sister (she was my mother's oldest child), whose skin was tan brown and hair was thick, soft and wavy-straight, especially affirmed my beauty and that I, my mother's youngest child, was special. For reasons that I can't fully explain, my general impression was that white people liked brown skin Black people best. As a child, I didn't have much contact with white people, they were on TV, and they were the teachers when I started school. As a pre-adolescent and teenager, I knew the white people that my parents worked with. My mother was an LPN, and my father was the floor manager of a steel mill. When my brother Ronald was in Vietnam, three of his (southern) white fellow soldiers stayed with us for a day before catching their connecting flight. He never told us they were white, but my mom guessed just before leaving for the airport to pick them up.

By now, we lived in a large house with four bedrooms and two staircases. My mother was especially fond of the hardwood parquet floors. They were meticulously cared for, always perfectly shining. It was one of those neighborhoods that opened to Blacks in the wake of the Civil Rights Movement. For me, our block was long, with trees at one end and hot summer sun at the other. I lived at the sunny end of the block, and, in remembering it, Stephen and I may have been the only kids who played with the children at both ends. A couple of doors away, on the same side of the street as me, there was another brown-skinned Black girl whose hair was always straightened. Her name was Joanne. Her father was a doctor, and her mother an alcoholic. She had an older brother who was in college. My mom hesitated to allow me to go into Joanne's house, but I was the only child on the block that Joanne was allowed to be friends with. Also, at the sunny end, but across the street, were two very tall but not much older than me sisters, Kathy and Dianne. They were what Black people would call "thick." They lived with the mother, grandmother and an older brother

38 *Feeling Race*

who, like Joanne's brother, was in college. He had gotten all of the family's good looks. Kathy, Dianne and Joanne all went to Catholic school. At the shady end of the block, there were two households with children. There was an extended family household on the same side of the street as Kathy and Dianne. There were two girls who were my age, Veronica and Cassandra. They always wore dresses. While Joanne and I wore our hair in braids, unless it was a special occasion, their hair was always curled. I would go over to talk to Veronica and Cassandra, but they were not allowed off of the porch, so they didn't actually get to play with the other kids on the block. The other house at the shady end of the street was on the same side as mine. It was a family of six kids. The two oldest were girls, Denise and Teresa. They were followed by three brothers, and the youngest was a girl. In comparison to the other households, they were poor. One of their parents worked at night, and the other during the day. I never actually saw either of them, but Denise and Teresa were in charge. I would spend hours playing in front of their house, most often jumping double-dutch.

Besides the big houses, another plus of the neighborhoods was that a brand new elementary school had been built. In fourth or fifth grade, I made friends with a white girl who was bused to my school. Standing alone in the school yard during recess, she truly looked absolutely frightened. I remember my mother's opposition to my being bussed. In her words, she "raised hell" to insure that I was not bused to a school in a poor white neighborhood. I don't know exactly where it was that she "raised hell," but I think it was at the white school. I remember what looked like sorrow on the faces of the Black kids as the school buses pulled up to my school at the end of the day. I think that I thought that white people like brown skin Black people best because we were easily identified. Light skin black people like my mother were somehow a problem. Though, as a child who was still in elementary school, I could not have explained white racial dominance; I could not have called it white supremacy. Even though I was certain of my family's love for me, even though I was certain of my beauty, my brown skin marked me. I lived among those who were "Black like me," but I felt the implications of whiteness and its ramifications for my blackness.

When I turned 14, I was finally allowed to ride the subway and bus by myself. My sister and her family had returned from Germany, where my brother-in-law, who was in the army, had been stationed. They were staying at my grandparents' house, and I was going to spend the weekend with them. My brother Ronald had insisted that I be allowed to wear mini dresses and had convinced my mother that it was okay for me to wear my hair in a huge Angela Davis-style afro. My body had begun to change from the lanky, skinny of childhood, foreshadowing the curves of womanhood. I came up the subway steps at what was then called Broad and Columbia, and today is Broad and Cecil B. Moore. I was wearing a navy blue spandex, spaghetti straps tank top

Feeling Race 39

and intricately patterned navy blue and white hot pants. I had on white thong sandals, and my fro was perfect. The brothers on the corner called out. It was before the age of "white feminism," and I had mastered the art of acknowledging without engaging, which protected me and respected them.

In the sway of my baby-girl, woman-to-be hips, the subtle bounce of my bra-less barely-there breast and the stomp of my very shapely legs, I felt the power that would carry me through. You see, I became the white girl on the playground, only in black. You see, I am the 4.0, 3.89 graduate student that my white peers did not want to partner with on projects. I am the one who was never told about the study group. I am the university professor on the campus at Broad and Cecil B. Moore, the one where I came in that summer of my fourteenth year to see the Black Panther Party, Sonia Sanchez and Nikki Giovanni, whose retirement is at hand but collegiality has always been a shadow. I felt my race that summer, as I feel it now – in the swirl of BLACK POWER, clenched fist and BLACK IS BEAUTIFUL – I am the breath of the 1960s.

Vaso

Feeling Race as a Greek Ethnic

As I reflect on my life and the influence the racial structure in the US has had on it, I see a story about a child of Greek immigrants wanting to be American and identifying with the white ethnic children in her neighborhood. I learned about the everyday practice of racial privilege and experienced its pain as my Greek community and parents rejected me and my choices of a Black boyfriend as a college girl and later an interracial marriage. I never really thought of my whiteness in the way a person of color would theirs, I suppose, given the trauma of being Black and Brown in America. This familial conflict highlighted the boundaries of race for me and my immigrant family. My studies in sociology, starting in 1982, empowered me with new knowledge to understand race in America and my privileged place in it. The normative nature of whiteness clouded my understanding of this privilege. At the same time, I was drawn to my Greekness since I grew up in a community with strong ethnic networks.

Greek Bubble

As a young girl in the 1970s, I stood inside of my *Greekness*, where Americans, in my mind, consisted of the white ethnics in my NYC neighborhood. The newer immigrants on the block, such as my Greek family and the Italian shoe maker next door, were part of a multicultural segment set apart from the earlier Americanized Irish and German immigrants, who had settled in the neighborhood for decades. I wanted to become more like my Americanized neighbors. There was an invisible wall between the Americans and my Greek

40 *Feeling Race*

Figure 1.5 Vaso in Greek school, sixth grade
Source: Photographer unknown

life. This was my first understanding of *difference,* and I wanted to be a part of this American world.

During those early years, I attended a Greek Orthodox parochial school and, aside from a Filipino and a Colombian girl on my block that I sometimes played with, all my friends were Greek from Greek school, and every weekend was spent socializing with my Greek cousins. By the late 1970s, I had started attending the local American high school. It was these coveted Americans of my imagination that became my friends. This was the group that I went to high school with: Irish and German American-born children who had grown up in this predominantly Irish neighborhood of Queens. Hannah, Katie and Cara would become my best friends in high school. We would skip school to attend the St. Patrick's Day parade. I would come to love the music of Janis Joplin, Neil Young, Chick Correa and Grover Washington. Becoming American, for me, meant listening to Rock and Roll and Jazz and hanging out with my white ethnic friends. I was drawn to a progressive America reflected in popular music and culture of the 1970s.

America represented a safe place for me. In my imagination, it was the place where girls have dreams. It was the place where I could be heard without the backlash of my mother's anger and the assault of her wooden spoon. I felt afraid, powerless and alone in my family, but I had the promise of America and its feminist suggestion to hold on to.

Feeling Race   41

Closer to Whiteness

I attended the State University of New York in Binghamton in 1983, yet I was in a precarious mental and social space since leaving home as an unmarried young Greek woman shamed my mother. This new experience and independence suggested new ways of seeing the world. During that time, aside from a picture on my childhood bedroom wall of a Black boy and white girl holding hands, I never interacted with Black people until my second year in college when I moved off campus.

My college dorm was a microcosm of the racial and ethnic structure of NYC, composed of mostly Jewish, Irish, German and Italian students; my roommate was a Dominican girl from Washington Heights. I didn't understand then that my early friendships with the Irish and German girls were shaped by racial forces that, to me, were evasive. It was an Italian American student from upstate New York who came to be my best friend and opened my eyes to race relations in America. She inspired me to read Alex Hailey's (1966) *Autobiography of Malcolm X*, Eldridge Cleaver's (1968) *Soul on Ice* and Karl Marx's (2015) *The Communist Manifesto*. In those college days, I read Toni Morrison's (1970, 1973) *The Bluest Eye* and *Sula*, Alice Walker's (1976) *Meridian*, Maya Angelou's (2009) *I Know Why the Caged Bird Sings* and Zora Neal Hursten's (2018) *Their Eyes Were Watching God*. I was drawn to the humanity of the characters in these great works and to the hardships of the Southern women. I felt the pain of women's oppression and Black oppression all mixed up with mine.

I moved off campus for my second year in college and fell in love with the boy next door. I was insanely in love, yet everything about him was foreign to me then. His black skin, self-assurance, stocking cap and the smell of Dax on his hair. Even before my mother knew about my boyfriend, I was gripped by my mother's terror; for having shamed my body, Greek girl modesty and the white race she was evasively connected to. As a student of sociology, I developed a critical perspective of race and gender, and this ideology gave me a new way of being in the world. As I moved away from my family in space and ideology, my ethnicity mattered less, and being white came into focus. This whiteness, once evasive, became clear, given my studies and new love and its consequences.

Family Racism

I was punished by my family for having a Black boyfriend. I was afraid. I still carry the pain and its effective shadows. My forgiveness of the perpetrators is apprehensive and laden with painful past experiences when I see them, yet I smile humbly because I love them. I became more and more emotional around issues of race, gender and violence. I remember, as a young teacher, how I cried because of the racial tension at our school during the OJ Simpson trial. It was

42 *Feeling Race*

a day when one of our counselors and I were at a secret war over who killed Nicole Simpson. The media pictures of Nicole's bruised face and my memories set me in opposition to my friend. I remember feeling like the white outsider and bursting into tears in our faculty and staff meeting that day.

Interracial Love

I remember the first day I met my husband. It was the mid-1990s, and I was a new teacher competing with the veterans by the machine to make copies for my upcoming class. One of them was schooling me on how to do this and that. Behind him stood a dark-skinned man with eyes the size of oceans. I was drawn into those waters by my own projection of who I was and what I hoped for. When I first started dating my husband, my father-in-law wondered about me; my mother-in-law, with pleasure, noted my doting on her son; his sisters and female cousins gave me the cold shoulder, testing me to figure out if my love was real. I remember flying home early from a family reunion of theirs, feeling like an outsider and crying in my coffee. Yet I understood the reaction of my new family's discomfort came from their understanding and living race in America, from a concern for and, maybe, possessiveness of their son, brother or cousin. It didn't come from that angry place of white anger. They didn't stay apprehensive about me for long since; my Greek girl doting behavior pleased them. Until the end of his life, my father-in-law would routinely share the same funny incident with me about a tourist he observed while traveling in Greece, who, burdened by a heavy backpack, fell into the water from a small fishing boat.

Despite my education in race relations and my racialized experiences, I still had a naivete about racism; I was tainted by racial neoliberalism and the romanticism of multiculturalism. For example, when in 1999, my husband and I bought a home in a white ethnic neighborhood in Queens, New York, I was in denial about how the white neighbors might react. I still considered America a safe place to be, ideologically and in my new neighborhood. Soon after we moved in, we were accused of renting out our basement, which is illegal in that part of town. We first received a letter from the community board informing us of our alleged infraction. I remember the letter was addressed by someone who wrote in a European style of lettering. I thought my mother might have written the letter, given the style of writing, to ruin my relationship. We never planned to rent any part of our new home.

When my mother-in-law came to visit us in our new home, for the first time, I was again shaken by a racist neighbor. He was a developmentally challenged adult son of an elderly woman two houses down the street. As my beautiful brown-skinned mother-in-law stepped out of her car, this man came darting out into the sidewalk, gesticulating and trying to get his words out and said, "We don't like these people here." I was confused; I thought I misheard. I rushed my mother-in-law into my home to protect her from the affront.

Feeling Race 43

As the wife of a Black man, my fear rises every morning as I lie awake and cry out in my first prayer to God to keep him safe and above his enemies as he travels to work. I fear that if he were pulled over by a police officer for any reason, his words or tendency to get surly might be misconstrued by an officer and he might get thrown in jail or worse.

As a white woman, I am privileged. Yet I am pulled by my immigrant story, tugged by my Greekness. This might have more to do with the power that Greek families have over their children, but, for me, family and ethnicity are all mixed together. My mother and father were born, raised and married in Greece. Greek was my first language and the ethnicity of my lifelong friends. Despite the cruelty of my Greek ethnic family and my white identification, being Greek is a meaningful part of who I am.

Conclusion

Each of the authors demonstrated that race is a phenomenon, a fact, an existence. Race is something that is experienced and felt. It is taught in silence and with speech by both action and inaction. It is a mechanism that provides for safety and a tool for instilling danger and fear. As children, all the authors learned the boundaries of Blackness and whiteness, the meanings and the dangers of race. For Vaso, Greek ethnicity is a permeable boundary into whiteness. For Mary, whiteness is a lens for witnessing and addressing oppression against those who are Black/not white. Adriana is similarly positioned by the activism of her parents and her own experiences that demarcate the boundary between her and whites. For Donna-Marie, the traumas of being a Black child in a virtually all-white environment are stark, devastating and silencing. For Michelle, the opportunities afforded by residential and school integration are real. Yet the implications of her blackness never fade into the background; they are always there, marking her identity.

The authors, as is the case in general, received no formal training in "race" as they grew into adulthood and became academics and sociologists. Yet they came to know the "rules of race" in childhood, and they negotiated them across their lives. They recognized the power and resources of whiteness as well as the less-than and otherness of Blackness. Their reflections in this chapter demonstrate that they are all aware, regardless of their race, of the racial hierarchy from white to not quite white to Black. Moreover, they carry their experiences and this knowledge with them into their classrooms.

References

Albright, Matthew. 2016. "Wilmington Has a Long, Messy, Education History." *The Wilmington News Journal*, June 10.

Angelou, Maya. 2009. *I Know Why the Caged Bird Sings*. New York, NY: Ballantine Books.

44 *Feeling Race*

Bailey v. State, 363 A.2d 312. Supreme Court of Delaware. 1976.

Cleaver, Eldridge. 1968. *Soul on Ice.* New York, NY: Random Publishing Group.

Do the Right Thing. 1989. Written by Spike Lee. 40 Acres and a Mule Filmworks.

Fear of a Black Planet. 1990. Public Enemy. Def Jam, Columbia.

Grahame, Kenneth, and Ernest Shepard. 1961. *The Wind and the Willows.* New York, NY: Scribner.

Howell, Jordan. 2020. "The Peach Tree: Part I: Sunday." *Delaware Today,* July 22. Accessed August 17, 2023.

———. 2020. "The Stunning Second Part of Sheila Ferrell's Tragic Story: The Protests, Part II: Monday, August 18 to Friday, September 5, 1975." *Delaware Today,* September 1.

Hurston, Zora Neale. 2018. *Their Eyes Were Watching God.* Virago Modern Classics. London, UK: Virago Press.

The Jeffersons. 1975–1985. Created by Don Nicholl, Michael Ross, and Bernie West. T.A.T. Communications Company and Embassy Television.

Marx, Karl, and Friedrich Engels. 2015. *The Communist Manifesto.* London: Penguin Books.

Morrison, Toni. 1970. *The Bluest Eye.* New York, NY: Holt, Rinehart and Winston.

———. 1973. *Sula.* New York, NY: Knopf Publishing Group.

Omi, Michael, and Howard Winant. 1986. *Racial Formation in the United States: From the 1960s to the 1980s.* New York, NY: Routledge.

Roots: The Saga of An American Family. 1977. Written by Alex Haley. Wolper Productions.

Starpoint. 1985. *Object of My Desire.* Written by Ernesto Phillips, Keith Diamond, and Ky Adeyemo. Elektra Records.

Walker, Alice. 1976. *Meridian.* San Diego, CA: Harcourt Brace Jovanovich.

The White Shadow. 1978–1981. Created by Bruce Paltrow. MTM Enterprises.

X, Malcolm, and Alex Haley. 1966. *The Autobiography of Malcolm X.* London, UK: Hutchinson.

2 Teaching Race

Teaching race classes is a balancing act. As we stand at the front of our classrooms, we are caught in a conundrum. We must be true to the history and current social circumstances that are more likely than not to define the quality of life and experiences that are associated with different racial groups. In our efforts, we are faced with two distinctive conundrums. We are informing our students that race identities are not neutral. Moreover, in addressing the social realities that are associated with racial groups, we demonstrate to them the persistence of race-based social inequalities. In other words, we are teaching them the multiple ways that race does matter in our society. That is, we are illustrating the ways that their race might shape their quality of life. We hope that our efforts will prepare our students for the realities and challenges that are associated with race-based social inequalities. Yet we are not just telling our students about the realities of racism; we are reminding ourselves.

Adriana

In the late 1990s, I started teaching at Temple University as a young woman graduate student of color – I was 26 at the time – and in 2001, I was hired into a tenure track position at Delaware Community College (DCCC). When I was hired at DCCC, I was told I would be working with 18 men and that no women had ever been hired in the department because they could not find any that were "qualified." I was told that the search committee thought I was more than equipped to "handle" the men, and was therefore offered the job.

I primarily teach Experiences in Diversity and Introduction to Sociology classes, and in both courses, I focus on stratification, whiteness and resistance. I have dedicated my life to increasing folks' awareness of racism; challenging inequity; teaching social activism; and developing and implementing policies to create a more equitable society. Although my social justice work extends well beyond the parameters of the classroom, my teaching contract requires that I teach ten classes per year. I also teach several overload classes and spend a lot of time evaluating and fine-tuning my teaching.

DOI: 10.4324/9781003442448-3

46 *Teaching Race*

Teaching sociology-based race classes which center whiteness as problematic is complicated for a variety of reasons. In regard to my identity, I am petite, racially ambiguous and female. My identities cause concern, and I am resisted for existing and talking about racism (Harlow 2003; Pittman 2010; Tuitt et al. 2009). Other factors which complicate teaching about race include: (1) most people are not taught to think about society on a macro level, where behaviors and actions are shaped by institutions, (2) some students do not believe racism exists, and (3) faculty often lack the time and resources necessary to process – and recover from – the emotional toll extracted from classes centering racism (Cazenave 2014). In the following sections, I will discuss these reasons and then conclude with techniques I have used to try and increase student engagement.

I. *Difficulty of Teaching Race Studies: Macro Structures*

First, teaching about racism in "whiteness-centered" courses from a sociological perspective is challenging because, as a society, we are socialized to think about societal issues on a micro (individual) level, not a macro (institutional) level. We are NOT taught to consider the impact of social institutions on group behavior and the ways in which systems create and perpetuate inequality. Since sociology focuses on how macro structures create group-based injustice and inequality and then shifts to what we can do, through organizing and public policy initiatives (again, macro level engagement), to create more equitable and less oppressive social conditions, students are constantly being asked to examine the world from a new and challenging perspective. Encouraging students to reflect on how systems shape and impact group behavior regarding inequality demands that they shift their thinking from "individual-based" motives and consequences to "group-based" impacts and outcomes. This mind shift is an active exercise, and it is as difficult to teach as it is for students to grasp.

Figuring out how to persuade students to think about racism from a macro-sociological perspective was especially hard at the start of my teaching career. Some students had difficulty understanding the "macro" view of the world, while others refused to believe that any factors beyond the individual's choices affected *group* outcomes.

My teaching at this point revolved heavily around lecturing about the different racial and ethnic groups coming to the USA, discussing the models of assimilation, and focusing on the work of Comte, Marx, DuBois and Omi and Winant. In teaching race, I tried to incorporate concrete examples into my lectures to illustrate the impact of social institutions on behavior and actions. As interesting as I thought the material was, I began to realize that the connections I was trying to make between historical macro structures, social theorists and racism were simply not working.

I cannot explain the tediousness of reciting 90-minute lectures on macro structures and their impact on group behavior with the realization that many

Teaching Race   47

students were not paying attention, were having difficulty understanding what I was trying to teach and/or could not relate the material on macro structures to their daily lives. This realization came as I acknowledged to myself that the lack of student participation was more about what I was doing than student apathy. My early teaching strategy left me exhausted, and I had to re-evaluate it.

II. Difficulty of Teaching Race Studies: Racism Still Exists

Second, teaching racial stratification to primarily white students is challenging because many students raised in a neoliberal climate believe the worst of racism is behind us. Some cling to the perspective that racial inequity is rooted in the past and that there is no such thing as contemporary racism. As a result, teaching *about* whiteness begins from the point of contention. We do not begin from a place of neutrality or acceptance; we start on the battlefield of white denial and fragility.

As a society, we have been taught to be uncomfortable analyzing inequality for many reasons because we have been fed the myth of meritocracy: hard work alone can lift us up, regardless of one's race. The material I teach directly contradicts the idea of the "American Dream" and points to race as a continued barrier to opportunity for people of color. We do not live in a post-racial era. Not only is this challenge to the idea of "freedom and liberty for all" complicated for some students on a philosophical level, but information that belies this idea can also cause students stress because they are challenged to rethink their current perspectives and their past racial socialization.

Student discomfort, however, does not mean that we should "avoid controversial matters" but that teachers should deliberately keep them at the center of classroom instruction. Nonetheless, information which exposes contradictions in the American system is, at times, especially hard for students to process, especially for those who possess at least one dominant group status. These are the students that I have worked hard to retain because they are too often the students who disengage and drop the class.

Teaching courses on inequity garner serious conversation; intense reflections on one's social upbringing; thoughts about whether one is comfortable with how one was raised; and deep questions on the structure of opportunity allocation. Some students are surprised by what we learn; some become angry; some feel sad and cry; some feel defensive; and others feel enthusiastic because they finally find the language and theoretical context to understand and explain what they have felt/experienced for a long time. Teaching students that racism still exists, when from K-12 they have been taught we are "beyond" race and that there has always been – and continues to be – racial disequilibrium in the USA based on America's "possessive investment in whiteness" is indeed a formidable task (Haltinner 2014).

48 *Teaching Race*

III. Difficulty of Teaching Race Studies: Time, Resources and Processing Content

Third, there is a lot of content to cover in a sociology of race and racism class. As such, we often run out of time to discuss all the material assigned. We also often lack the time to *process* the information by reflecting on – and sifting through – early socialization, the ensuing feelings evoked by the literature and the emotionality triggered by the content. The lack of time and resources often makes race courses feel like an unfinished project.

When we move through the material quickly, students often do not have the time to process the content and how they feel about it. Therefore, I sometimes "lose" students. When students do not have ample time to think about and then talk about the material, they engage with the material a little less personally. That is, when I rush through the material because we also must cover the next section before an exam, students may not have adequate time to make the connections between the material and their lives and their participation in the "racial contract." This can result in students feeling overwhelmed by the material and ultimately by the class.

I want students to be receptive to learning the material I teach, even if they do not agree with the content. As such, this question of "reaching" students has plagued me throughout my entire teaching career. Since we (humans) are often unable to achieve our full potential because we are not given the space, support or encouragement to fully process all our emotions and, as a result, those emotions block our full intelligence, we must design the space to do this emotional labor in the classroom, with our students, regardless of how uncomfortable it is (Kim 2016). When one is exposed to sensitive information, it might re-stimulate old emotional hurts, pains and trauma, including (but not limited to): pain, suffering, confusion, denial, anger, resentment, blame, guilt, defensiveness, fear, sadness and shame. When these emotions are stimulated, and a person has no safe, supportive or comfortable place to process them, learning can be reduced and impaired because one's mind is focused on the emotion stimulated. Furthermore, once one is "triggered," one may engage in unconventional behavior, such as refusing to talk in a classroom. As such, it is critically important to process student emotions so that they can focus on learning.

Thinking about the role of emotions in teaching and learning, I realized that I had very strong and personal reactions to certain topics in the classes I taught and that my responses were culturally grounded. Getting to the reason for, or the root of, the expression of emotion is what I believe is critical. It is not the response that is interesting to me, it is the reason for the response, and I often feel that I do not get to this critical point in the classroom: the point of figuring out why students respond the way they do to material we cover. My reflection on this dynamic of how and why we respond the way we do and why it is important to get to the reasons for our responses made me realize that if I, a grown woman with a PhD, was stimulated so quickly by course content and

Teaching Race 49

did not have the time to process those feelings, there was no way my students were not being "triggered" by some of the topics covered in class as well. Using this analysis to consider student success in the classroom, I asked myself how student emotions could impact their own learning (Bryan 2016).

This made me do a full stop and rethink my teaching. I have worked hard to create a safe and inclusive classroom environment because I have often felt like an outsider in classrooms. However, while I was reading about the role of emotions in teaching and learning, I suddenly realized I was probably unintentionally "triggering" students, and thus my classroom may not have been as "safe" or inclusive as I would have liked it to be. I had never thought about the emotionality in education, and I realized this is a very real thing.

As a professor, I am committed to examining the relationship between processing emotions and effective teaching when it comes to racial inequality. Historically, emotions have been viewed by sociologists as a dependent variable (product of social influences), but over the last 30 years, there is a new understanding of "emotions" as an independent variable, especially when it comes to "problems in substantive fields as diverse as gender roles, stress, small groups, social movements, and stratification (Thoits 1989)." As such, I am interested in thinking about how structural inequality exhibits itself in interpersonal interactions by focusing on how our anxieties, resentments and anger impact learning about social issues and stratification. That is, I want to explore what sociocultural factors and processes influence our understanding of our own as well as others' emotional experiences. How are power and status tied to certain emotions and how is this equilibrium impacted within a stratification course? That is, I am interested in the correlation between emotion awareness or "discharge" and effective teaching.

Historically, when it comes to teaching students information and knowledge in classrooms, we begin with the idea that knowledge is "emotion-free" and painless. As a result, we have not created an education system with intentional structures designed to recognize, accept and work through difficult emotions or the pain that comes with learning specific content (Matias, Henry, and Darland 2017). Since we now know that learning is an emotionally fraught experience, I want to figure out how to best teach information that is challenging and which may "trigger" students. That is, I am interested in devising strategies to teach through the pain and discomfort and to help students not only process their emotions but the impact of their peers' emotions as well.

It is very important to find ways to effectively communicate with people about race and racism and help students process emotions they may experience, which may impede learning, so that we can begin to tackle and decrease the socially constructed differences that make us feel estranged from one another. We have more in common with one another than we know – and I want to find better ways of communicating this with students. Understanding our common humanity by processing emotions that may interfere with learning about race in race classes is critical.

50 *Teaching Race*

IV. Adding Revolutionary Theory and Social Movement Literature to the Curricula

In the attempt to get students to recognize that macro structures are relevant to their own lives, that racism still exists and to ensure we have time to process content, I continuously attempt to improve my classes. In this effort, I have: (1) included more in-class activities which illustrate the direct impact between students' daily lives and macro structures, such as unemployment, health care and mass incarceration; (2) assigned material on revolutionary theory and resistance; and (3) reduced the number of assigned readings so we have more time to process content and address emotions. This pattern of attempting to improve the class is a perpetual wheel in motion.

When I taught about racism initially, I felt I had to "prove" that contemporary racism existed. I taught American history, racial theory, discrimination and privilege, public policy and the law. Additionally, I critically examined and showcased the concerted violence levied against Black and Brown people by the state. I talked about enslavement; Jim Crow; segregation; lynching; rape; forced sterilization; medical experiments performed on Black and Brown folks in prisons by the government; the impact of policy-driven structural violence in areas such as housing, health care and employment; multiple systems of racial domination; generational trauma, etc.

These were violent and exhausting lectures. At times I felt like I had to "break" my students for them to accept the reality of racism. I did this in various ways and often felt as if I was (re)traumatizing my students, especially my students of color, and myself, in this process.

The content of domestic terrorism weighed heavily on all of us because teaching – and learning – about racism is spirit-breaking. During my lectures, I crushed optimism. I saw students cry in their chairs. And this was not just my students of color; many of my white students were also horrified by America's racism. Nonetheless, I knew it was critically important to teach this information so that they understood America's love affair with racism.

I wanted students to understand the urgency of racism, but I also wanted to leave them excited, optimistic and motivated to resist. I did not want them to be depressed, frustrated and alienated. As I focused more on how I taught, I considered ways to get my students involved and active.

I did this in various ways. For instance, I created my own PowerPoints. I used bullets to highlight concepts and theories and incorporated a plethora of visually stunning and colorful images into my work. I added murals, paintings, graffiti, faces, video clips and music to my lectures. I included student voices and examples of resistance. I showered them with examples of multi-racial coalition building and activism.

I also sought out and developed in-class activities that focused on students' lives. I decided to use more current readings for class. I moved away from a traditional textbook to a contemporary anthology – *Race, Class and Gender in the United States*, edited by Rothenberg – which incorporated marginalized

Teaching Race 51

voices, short stories, personalized narratives, actual laws/policies and illuminated humanity, dignity, agency and group empowerment.

Now we begin from the premise that racism exists; I present historical and contemporary documents which clearly illustrate state-designed racist policies; I develop worksheets for student use, including a general worksheet to encourage them to learn about individual, organizational and institutional racism; and we identify people and social movements which have resisted American oppression and dehumanization. Here are a few examples of revolutionaries, films, documentaries and books I incorporated into my lectures:

Revolutionaries

Queen Nanny aka "Granny Nanny" (1686–1733)

Born in Ghana
Enslaved in Jamaica
Led a community of formerly enslaved Africans called the Windward
    Maroons
Maroons were enslaved in the Americas and escaped and formed
    independent settlements
Fought a multiyear war against the British colonizers in Jamaica
Raid the plantations at night to take machinery and free people
She had a bounty placed on her head
1976 Jamaica declared her their only female national hero
She was a leader, military tactician and strategist
She is on the Jamaican $500 bill

Ida B. Wells (1862–1931)

Small woman
Journalist
Wrote about and fought against lynching!
Owned a gun/advocated Black gun ownership to ward off white terrorists

Soledad Chacon (1890)

First Latina elected to a statewide office in the US
Elected Secretary of State for New Mexico in 1922

Lolita Lebron (1919–2010)

Puerto Rican Nationalist
Wanted freedom for Puerto Rico
Against US colonization
Shot up US Congress to free her people
Was convicted of attempted murder and other crimes after leading an assault
    on the US House of Reps (1954)
"I didn't come to kill. I came to die."

52   *Teaching Race*

Dolores Huerta (1930)

> Farm-worker
> Engaged in boycotts, picketing, protesting and lobbying
> Forced the creation of legislation (laws) to protect immigrants

Kathleen Cleaver (1945)

> Involved in the Black Power Movement
> Communications Secretary for the Black Panther Party (joined Nov. 1967)
> Two-thirds of the Black Panther Movement were comprised of women
> She was the first woman to be part of the party's decision-making body

Judith Baca (1946)

> Muralist
> Painted the great wall of Los Angeles 1976–1984
> One half-mile mural that told the story of Chicanos in Los Angeles

Sylvia Rivera (1951–2002)

> Fought for LGBTQ rights, homeless people and people of color
> Identified as a drag queen
> Active with the Gay Liberation Front

Bree Newsome (1985)

> From North Carolina
> Activist and filmmaker who engaged in civil disobedience
> June 27, 2015, she scaled a pole at the South Carolina State House and removed the Confederate flag
> Her act resulted in publicly pressuring state officials to remove the Confederate flag on June 10, 2015

Sophia Cruz (2010)

> When she was 5, in 2015, she started her fight against deportation
> "I want to tell you that my heart is very sad, because I'm scared that, one day, ICE [Immigration and Customs Enforcement] is going to deport my parents. I have the right to live with my parents. I have the right to be happy."

Revolution and Resistance Films and Documentaries

1. *The Murder of Fred Hampton* (1971)
2. *Norma Rae* (1979)
3. *For Us, the Living: The Medgar Evers Story* (1983)
4. *Matewan* (1987)
5. *Malcolm X* (1982)

Teaching Race 53

6. *At the River I Stand* (1983)
7. *Erin Brockovich* (2000)
8. *A Huey P. Newton Story* (2001)
9. *Trudell* (2005)
10. *Walkout* (2006)
11. *The Story Behind the Image: Salute* (2008)
12. *Che': Part I and Part II* (2008)
13. *The Black Power Mixtape 1967–1975* (2011)
14. *Mama Africa* (2011)
15. *Mandela: Long Walk to Freedom* (2013)
16. *Cesar Chavez* (2014)
17. *Selma* (2014)
18. *What Happened, Miss Simone?* (2015)
19. *This Changes Everything* (2015)
20. *Black Panthers: Vanguard of the Revolution* (2015)
21. *Moonlight* (2016)
22. *13ᵗʰ* (2016)
23. *Dolores* (2017)
24. *Baltimore Rising* (2017)
25. *The Young Karl Marx* (2018)
26. *ReMastered: The Two Killings of Sam Cooke* (2019)
27. *Dark Waters* (2019)
28. *Harriet* (2019)
29. *Who Killed Malcom X?* (2020)

Books

1. *Pushout* by Monique W. Morris
2. *The New Jim Crow* by Michelle Alexander
3. *Just Mercy* by Bryan Stevenson
4. *Between the World and Me* by Ta-Nehisi Coates
5. *Angela Davis Autobiography* by Angela Davis
6. *A People's History of the United States of America* by Howard Zinn
7. *Lies my Teacher Taught Me* by James Loewen
8. *White Fragility* by Robin DiAngelo
9. *River, Cross My Heart* by Breena Clarke
10. *Pedagogy of the Oppressed* by Paulo Freire
11. *Medical Apartheid* by Harriet A. Washington
12. *How to be Less Stupid about Race* by Crystal Marie Fleming
13. *Begin Again* by Eddie Glaude

Incorporating revolutionaries, resistance and social movement content into my teaching captured students' attention and increased engagement. On the way to that place, however, I had to think about what makes a classroom

54   *Teaching Race*

dynamic and that led me to think about when and how I felt most energized by learning. Thinking about great teachers led me to my father. My dad, who was one of my teachers at Che'-Lumumba, is white, and he is an artist, a writer and a revolutionary. Thinking about him and the anti-racism work he has spent over 60 years doing – inside and outside of the classroom – made me remember that students like excitement and that you can capture their attention if you don't bore them to death. Stories that capture the enthusiasm of living, the risk of taking a chance and the joy of solidarity, bring energy, delight and optimism into teaching. I learned this from my father and I should never have forgotten it.

In the pursuit of energizing the classroom, I also remembered that it was important to include the stories of whites who were committed to social justice. My father taught me this as well. Incorporating these voices is important because: (1) students in K-12 settings are usually not taught about white allies, and (2) teaching about white resistance to oppression allows white students to see that they do not have to merely support the status quo. By including the activism of whites, students can see that they can choose allyship, resist oppression and fight for liberation. It is in this space that we begin to open doors and perhaps minds.

Here are examples of whites who resisted oppression and whom I include in my lectures:

1. Benjamin Lay (Quaker)
2. John Brown (Abolitionist)
3. Juliette Hampton Morgan (social activist prior to Montgomery Bus Boycott/ committed suicide)
4. Grimke sisters (anti-slavery suffragettes who ended up losing almost everything in the battle for racial equality and women's rights)
5. Albert Parsons (workers' rights advocate/convicted of conspiracy and hung)
6. Viola Liuzzo (killed by the KKK during the Civil Rights Movement)
7. Andrew Goodman (murdered by KKK during Freedom Summer)
8. Michael Schwerner (CORE, murdered by KKK during Freedom Summer)
9. James Ian Tyson (worked with Bree Newsome to take down Confederate Flag)

Including within the narrative of stratification the stories and examples of people-powered movements and cross-racial organizing efforts which have challenged systems of oppression is exciting and liberating, and I find students participate much more in class conversations when exposed to this content. Teaching resistance highlights that we are agentic and that we have the power to overthrow systems.

Teaching Race 55

Conclusion

Teaching race and racism courses is emotionally and physically exhausting and I think this is especially true when one possesses multiple "minority" statuses. I started teaching as a young woman in my mid-twenties and am now in my fifties. I have worked hard to try and become a better teacher and to improve what and how I present information. Over the years, the issues I have struggled with in the classroom include: (1) getting students to embrace a macro perspective, (2) getting students to realize that racism exists when neoliberalism espouses we are in a post-racial society, and (3) finding more time to process content and student emotions in the classroom.

I have not been able to wave a magic wand and make my classroom perfect. As I have become an older woman of color, when I face challenges and disengagement, I try to address them more calmly – perhaps in a way I have less to prove. I force myself to breathe every few seconds and am much more likely to respond with humor. The jokes are not about the student or the content; they are an attempt to break the tension. Furthermore, once I address the question or the "challenge" the student has posed, I move on with the lecture. I do not get stuck in the mud. That is, I do not spend an enormous amount of time going back and forth with my students. I respond to the comment and then I move on to the next item on the day's agenda. This approach has let me experience far less conflict in the classroom than in my early teaching.

Donna-Marie

Early Years Teaching Race Studies

Nervously, I sit in front of the chairperson of my department. She pulls out my teaching evaluations from a folder on her desk. I brace myself for the humiliation I am about to face, knowing this required year-end review of my teaching will be particularly harsh. I have read the comments of disgruntled students, comments often painful to hear. These were new course assignments that I naively agreed to teach that deal with the many complex issues of race. My commander-in-chief, the lady chairperson, begins to read selected indignant and irate student comments written about me on the evaluation forms distributed to them at the semester's end. I cringe.

> *"Dr. Peters won't let us talk."*
> *"Every time I try to answer a question, she shuts me down."*
> *"I'm not racist, but in front of the whole class, Dr. Peters implied that I am one."*
> *"The professor embarrasses us by dismissing what we have to say that [contradicts] what she has just stated as fact."*

56 *Teaching Race*

She looks at me, and I'm beginning to twitch. In a stern, sharp, British accent, she shouts, "You must let them speak! You must allow them to have a point of view! They must not be denied *Freedom of Speech*!" "Even if it's white supremacist speech," I shout back, not as a question but as a statement. "I think you know what I mean," she abruptly stops shouting, lowers her voice, gets up from her desk and walks toward the door. She turns the doorknob and slightly opens it so that the administrative assistant seated on the other side of the door can not only hear us but see us.

I have never been a physically violent person, and this was not the time to become one. I immediately pivoted to a performance of self-consciousness and self-control. My voice became a whisper. I apologized for my conduct in response to her extremely constructive criticism. I slowly rose to leave, convinced that it would be in my best interest to find a career outside of toxic teaching in the ivory tower. I took a deep breath in resignation as I slowly walked toward the open door. Suddenly, as if the sky opened up, I heard a sweet voice behind me say, "On a more positive note, the students say you care about them!"

Can We Talk? *A Monthly Workshop on Teaching Race*

Mimicking the accusatory tone of student voices, I read out loud what I have pulled up on the screen for an audience of teachers and administrators in the room to view:

> "*My uncle didn't get a city job. Because of affirmative action, they had to hire a Black person.*"
> "*I am white, and I don't have white privilege. We are trailer trash.*"
> "*My father's a policeman. They always get a bad rap.*"

I am conducting a monthly workshop on teaching race called *Can We Talk?* which I introduced to the Teaching and Learning Center and co-founded and co-facilitated for approximately ten years. In this workshop, I begin by announcing to the group of professors quietly attentive and seated around tables that allow for conversation: "Today's workshop is titled: *Understanding Ourselves in the Classroom.*" I then explain that I initiated this monthly workshop and began co-facilitating it with the director of the Teaching and Learning Center, having learned from the different teaching workshops that I had attended in the past of the need among many of my colleagues teaching issues of race in different disciplines to explore best practices in this area. I had been finding teaching this course on race very difficult and believed if I had a community with colleagues who wanted to improve their teaching in this area, together we could discuss our problems and together find solutions.

Teaching Race   57

I point to the screen and say, "When students say things like this in my classes, I would say what you just said sounds racist." Approximately 90% of the students that I was teaching in this course were taking this course solely because it is a graduation requirement. Most students in attendance had never taken a course on race. Like the insensitive race-related microaggressions professors inflict on students, I eventually came to realize upon self-reflection one day in a workshop that my knee-jerk comments were just as hurtful. What the students were hearing from me was their professor calling them a racist.

I enter the safe space of my classroom, repeating the words of my chairperson: "You can't shut them down!" Soon I am listening to students build bridges of understanding as they lead group discussions that follow rules of inclusive engagement. All voices heard! I see the surprise in the faces of students when I remain poised and unfettered, listening intently to a negative racial comment pour out of the mouth of a feeling-forgotten youth in this age of Trumpism, mis-information and the power of media.

Each semester, I work toward creating a learning experience for students that acknowledges their realities by meeting them where they are since I am keenly aware of the cognitive dissonance that students experience in race classes. I carefully scaffold assignments and class activities in a way that prepares students intellectually for each consecutive piece of new information. By asking students each week to place a racial lens on society, I tread slowly week by week through diverse course material, often challenging students to examine information that contradicts their beliefs. From the push-back that I receive from reluctant learners, I realize that for some of the students, having planted the seed will have to be enough. No spirit of democracy can exist in the classroom without diverse voices seated around the discussion table.

Empower their Voices

"Why do you imagine that talking about race is so difficult?" I pause, taking my time to look into the eyes of each of my students. The overwhelming number of them will be majoring in STEM, business and the health fields. There is an absence of diversity that is palpable in the experiences they receive in their neighborhood, school and religious environments. "We have topics under investigation that require critical examination from a myriad of perspectives. The best way to deepen our understanding of issues is through discussion and debate," I explain. Then, on the verge of desperation, I plead with my students, "Please don't hold back. Be open with me. Why doesn't anyone want to talk? I can't keep answering my own questions." I begin counting 1 . . . , 2 . . . , 3 . . . , 4 . . . , 5 . . .. A South Asian male, seated in the second row from the back to my left, raises his hand. I point in his direction and say his name. He exclaims, "I don't like to speak in any of my classes, not just this one."

58 *Teaching Race*

I respond with an understanding tone in my voice, saying, "It definitely takes a lot of self-confidence to answer questions in class." He responds affirmatively without hesitation, explaining, "Students measure your intelligence from what you say in class. I fear that what I say won't sound like I am very smart." I nod understandingly and state, "I appreciate what you just said, and can't thank you enough for breaking the ice." A white female student seated behind him immediately responds, "It is so embarrassing when the professor says your answer is wrong. So, why take the risk?" "You're right," I say, "That makes a lot of sense." Sensing that I am getting students to open up, I ask, "Are there other fears that students have that prevent them from talking in class?" A Black male student seated in the middle row in front of me responds, offering a teachable moment: "I fear being looked at as not as intelligent as other students in classes that I take because of my race. If I answer a professor's questions and my answer is wrong, I feel that I am confirming people's assumptions."

"We have a tortured relationship with race." I say to the class. Race is a taboo topic. We learn that it is politically incorrect to talk about race in public. How can I ask you to talk about race when talking about race is beyond the boundary of political correctness? I enter uncharted waters addressing the elephant in the room that no one wants to discuss: Race! I pointedly ask, "What do you fear will happen if you speak about race in class?" After a long silence, a white student unveils the juggernaut explaining, "Personally, I fear that what I say may be misunderstood." Spontaneously, the white female next to her emphatically exclaims, "And you are automatically labeled a racist. I have friends who are Black and friends of different races! I'm not a racist!"

"This is not a math class; there are no wrong answers! Whatever you say is contributing to an open-ended conversation," I repeat throughout the semester. New assignments are invented to empower student voices and to assuage their fears.

Last Lesson – Experiential Learning

I begin class by instructing the tapestry of multi-colored faces, "Please put away your cell phones so we can begin class. I can see when you are typing on your phone under your desks." I state as fact, in an instructional tone of voice, "Irish drink too much, and Italians are related to the mafia; Asians are good at math; and Blacks are good at sports." Students laugh. "What's so funny?" I feign ignorance, successfully gaining the attention of my audience. "No one buys into those ridiculous stereotypes today," a student responds. I say, "Really?"

I then proceed to cautiously take a deep dive into the sensitive waters of *privilege* and *implicit bias*. These are topics that I purposely save until the last two weeks of class, when students have 13 weeks of preparation to be ready to investigate this sensitive issue of race. "Most of us take privilege for granted," I say. (I abruptly change the topic from racial stereotyping to privilege with concerted effort and purpose). Next, I show a cartoon of a person in a wheelchair

Teaching Race 59

speaking about able-bodied privilege. I show a video titled *The Unequal Opportunity Race* (2020) that depicts a white male winning a race because of the history of societal obstacles that give him a competitive advantage and prevent his black male competitors from winning. I show a photo of two men holding hands that says, "Marriage is a privilege." I have the class play privilege bingo in which the intersectional social identities of students, including race, ethnicity, gender, cisgender, class and religion, are considered in the allocation of points. The white males win by a landslide. The two boys in the back cheer.

I announce with great enthusiasm: "Our invited guest speaker, Dr. Waidzunas from the sociology department, will now speak to us on his recent research in the area of race." Students immediately open their computers and notebooks to begin taking notes. Not a single student is texting under their desk. The two white boys in the back are demonstrating an unusual show of interest in the topic of race. "Thank you, Donna, for inviting me to speak to your class today." After referring to me by first name, even though I respectfully used the prefix Dr. when introducing him to the class, this dignified, professorially attired, spectacled, middle-aged white gentleman begins to lecture with a to-the-manner-born sense of entitlement.

From the very start of his lecture, Dr. Waidzunas botches the names of famous dead, white male sociologists. Smoothly and elegantly, this invited speaker reinvents sociological-sounding words and supports his argument with constant mumbo-jumbo, bedazzling the students. I look around to see if there are any perplexed faces in the room – not one. The two white boys in the back of the room are giving utmost attention to a topic they usually recoil from and find repugnant. Dr. Waidzunas concludes his remarks with a crescendo of convoluted words strung together, using malapropisms that sound like sociological jargon.

I ask the students if they have any comments. No one raises their hand. I thank Dr. Waidzunas, and he walks out the door. I then pass out a short survey asking students to evaluate Dr. Waidzunas' lecture. After quickly reading the completed surveys, I find what was to be expected. The professor's bumbling words, rambling sentences and meandering through a muffled illogical argument were not what each student heard. They heard what they saw: A respectable, highly credentialed, well-dressed, white male deserving high marks for his lecture's level of interest, clarity, organization, scholarly content and strength of argument. After reading the noncritical, glowing assessments provided by each student, I say to myself, "Now, what if you had given the exact same lecture?"

I repeat once again, "Most of us take privilege for granted." Emphatically, I say to the students, "The so-called scholarly talk you just heard made no sense at all. Although everyone gave Dr. Waidzunas 'excellent' for every aspect of his presentation, I hate to inform you, but what he said did not make any sense. Often, we can only see our true selves through the lens of experience. This experience has introduced us to the concept of *unconscious bias*." I look around the classroom to make certain that I have full attention, then emphatically state,

60 *Teaching Race*

"The stereotypes that we laughed at, think ridiculous and describe as obsolete, unconsciously remain within us. We have *unconscious bias* that is related to a person's social identity and connected to the issues of *privilege* and *non-privilege*. You gave Dr. Waidzunus what is called *white male privilege*." I pull-up on the screen a sociological definition of *privilege* to show the students. This, I hope, will minimize the damage this self-realization can do to the fragile egos seated in front of me. I conclude by strongly making the pronouncement: "No one is immune from having *unconscious, implicit bias*; It resides within us all!"

Mary

In teaching my first race classes, I was focused mostly on myself and my ego. My overriding goal was to be perceived as a white person who knew what they were talking about, so I spent an inordinate number of hours preparing for each class session. After gaining a modicum of confidence in myself, I began focusing more on content, but still content related to myself. I asked myself, "*What would have brought me out of the colorblind world I was in as a college student?*" The answer was not complicated. Though I didn't gain a color consciousness until after graduation, it was clear that what moved me was the inability to avoid the harsh realities I saw in images of the 1982 murder of Vincent Chin, the 1986 racist attack in Howard Beach, Queens, the 1991 police beating of Rodney King and countless other racist incidents I could no longer turn away from. I wanted them to see what I saw. I wanted to "hit them hard." More specifically, I wanted to "hit" *white* students with information that would make the presence of white supremacy irrefutable. I didn't think a whole lot about what students of color might need other than to hear a white person "telling it like it is." Not until 2013, 17 years after I began teaching, did I begin to seriously address what students of color might need and to reflect upon the movement power in the streets and the critical pedagogy in the classroom, and in that process of reflection, I came to the realization that all of my students need more than "hits," and that most of all, they need inspiration. They need to see themselves as potential activists, and as an activist myself committed to critical pedagogy, I need them to act.

1996–2013: Tough Lessons: **Hit Em Hard!**

Good morning students; here are today's numbers:

1982! Vincent Chin – *Probation for murder!*
1986! Howard Beach – *White mobs rule!*
1988! Willie Horton – *Dog-whistle politics, you see how it works?*
1989! Charles Stuart – *They killed my wife, not me!*
1991! Dubuque, Iowa – *Five crosses from the KKK!*
1992! Rodney King – *33 blows of innocence!*
1994! Denny's – *Jim Crow, alive and well!*

Teaching Race 61

Today's winning numbers again are: 1982, 1986, 1988, 1989, 1991, 1992 and 1994! White racism, white racism, white racism, white racism, white racism, white racism and white racism! Do you now see as I see? Of course you do! How could you not? Oh, is this difficult for you to hear? I'm sorry I didn't see you there, in your pain, your confusion and your suffering. Excuse me, please, as I'm trying to work through my own struggles, which require me to continue.

2000! Bush is President! – *600,000 Floridians Disenfranchised.*

2001! Everyone's a Suspect Now – *Balbir Singh Sodhi was shot down in Arizona.*

2002! One Strike and You're Out! – *63-year-old Barbara Hill is evicted from her home of 30 years because her grandson smoked a joint in the parking lot.*

2006! The Jena 6 – *The noose will not be criminalized.*

2008! *Hope?*

2011! *The State executes Troy Davis.*

2012! *George Zimmerman murdered Trayvon Martin.*

2013! *George Zimmerman is free.*

George Zimmerman is free. *This is what I've been trying to tell you!*

They heard me. I broke them. All of them. The white ones, the Black and Brown ones and the Yellow ones. There were always some students of color who fully adopted a neoliberal "colorblind" discourse, middle-class students taught by their parents to rise above racism and embrace meritocracy as a reality rather than a fantasy. Sometimes they came to see me. The pain in their voices and their postures was fresh. One Black student, in particular, came trembling. His very elite white boarding school had not prepared him. Everything we covered was hitting him like a ton of bricks. I had watched him wince in class on more than a few occasions. He didn't say much in my office. I think he came just to confirm that I was telling him the truth. The truth, something I was so set on sharing, had caused him great suffering. And at the time, I wasn't offering anything to ease that suffering.

2013–: Tough Lessons: Give Them Inspiration. Give Them a Choice

Their eyes lit up, their mouths opened, their chests pumped:

1838: *Angelina Grimke defied her slave-owning family, renounced her religion as a teenager, and appealed to Christian women to join the movement for abolition. She spoke in Pennsylvania Hall as the hordes threatened to burn it down – and did soon after her speech ended.*

1847: *Senator Corwin called on President Polk to leave Mexico alone! Stop this unjust war! Mexican lives matter!*

62   *Teaching Race*

1862: *Robert Smalls stole a Confederate ship, fought for the Union and bought his former slave owner's house for his mother. He then became one of many Reconstruction-era elected representatives. His mother OWNED the house where she was once enslaved!*

1877: *Wong Chin Foo called Jesus a "Johnny Come Lately" and invited White Anglo-Saxon Protestants to assimilate to Confucianism. Chinese must go? No, the Chinese Must Stay!*

1883: *Ida B. Wells, all five feet of her, refused to be removed from the train, took a bite out of the conductor's hand, sued for discrimination and won. 72 years before Rosa!*

1969: *Young Lords: Boricua is Awake! All Pigs Beware!*

2013: *Alicia Garza: #Black Lives Matter: A love letter to Black people.*

Black Lives Matter!
Black Lives Matter!
Black Lives Matter!
Black Lives Matter!

Smalls, Grimke, Chin Foo, Corwin, Wells, Garza and <u>insert your name here!</u>

Me: *What Can You Do? What Will You Have Done? You have a choice.*
Them: *But things are getting better!*
Me: *That's what Robert Smalls thought before he made a choice.*
Them: *But it's really getting better with every generation!*
Me: *Charlottesville was your people! My generation wasn't carrying tiki torches!*
Them: *But Trump...*
Me: *What Can You Do? What Will You Have Done? You have a choice. Make a choice.*
        The principles of equality, democracy and human morality were always available to those steering this ship, but they chose otherwise. They are available today! What do you choose? What. Do. You. Choose.

Choosing to Act?

I was putting them back together.

Students were reflecting on the resistance they were learning about:

We take for granted the radical movements that got us to this point in history, therefore forfeiting any vision of real progress for people of color. After consideration of our class discussions and struggling with my own thoughts

Teaching Race 63

and feelings, I have concluded that we still desperately need radical visions and movements (Black male student).

These discussions have led to my understanding of myself being one who can be considered an extremist against institutional racism (East Asian American female student).

I now understand that the consequences of that very history are the roots of racism today and are what motivate Kaepernick to believe that injustice still exists. It is now our responsibility to do what is in our power to end this continuing cycle of racism by refusing to be color-blind and acknowledging the past, present and future of racism (South Asian American female student).

Until this course taught me otherwise, I had thought that Africans rarely stood up and fought out of fear of horrific punishment. It may make me sound unintelligent to state that; however, I've learned about this era in relation to the white's iniquity alone. We are told to pity African Americans and wallow in guilt rather than do something about today's racism or learn from the past (white male student).

I am humbled, but it also spurs a desire in me to change our current status quo and to help influence our nation in a better direction (white male student).

They feel inspired. They see themselves as potential activists. But will they act?

Michelle

"Between me and the other world there is ever an unasked question: unasked by some through feelings of delicacy; by others through difficulties of rightly framing it. All, nevertheless, fluttering around it. They approach me in a half-hesitant sort of way, eye me curiously or compassionately and then instead of saying it directly, How does it feel to be a problem? They say, I know an excellent colored man in my town; or I fought at Mechanicsville; or, Do not these Southern outrages make your blood boil? At these I smile or am interested or reduce the boiling to a simmer, as the occasion may require. To the real question, How does it feel to be a problem? I seldom answer a word" (pg. 363).

"The history of the American Negro is the history of this strife, – this longing to attain self-conscious manhood, to merge his double self into a better and truer self. In this merging he wishes neither of the other selves to be lost. He would not Africanize America, for America has much to teach the world and Africa. He would not bleach his Negro soul in a flood of white Americanism, for he knows that Negro blood has a message for the world. He simply wishes to make it possible for a man to be both a Negro and an American, without being cursed and spit upon by his fellows, without having the doors of Opportunity closed roughly in his face" (Du Bois 1982, p. 365)

64　*Teaching Race*

As I was coming to the end of my PhD, my dissertation chair visited a class, The Black Community, that I taught. The purpose was to give me advice about my teaching because I was entering the job market. Although I had taught for years without this support from the faculty, my guess is that I would soon be representing The University, so it was time to make sure that I was getting it right. Although I am likely to sit at the front of the classroom now, either on the desk or in a chair, in those days, I would stand and eventually give into walking around the room. It was a technique that I used to keep my students' attention and to stop students from talking and other distracting behaviors. Also, it was a way of releasing tension and nervous energy. My chairperson sat towards the back of the room. Of course, I was very aware of his presence as I paced back and forth, delivering my lecture. At the end of the class, as the students were leaving, he came to the front of the room and said to me, "You are a very pedantic teacher." I was unfamiliar with the word, and I assumed that it had something to do with my pacing around the room. When I looked it up, I found out that word meant: one who is unimaginative or who unduly emphasizes minutiae in the presentation or use of knowledge; one who makes a show of knowledge; a formalist or precisionist in teaching. I could only wonder about the "why" of his statement. The course was titled *The Black Community*. Did my lecture consist of trivial details about the lives of African Americans and the sociological analysis of US race and ethnic relations? Or was this as close as he could get to acknowledging my expertise regarding the subject matter? How could I not be "pedantic"? I was, and very often have continued to be, caught in the debris, the minutiae, the shit of America's racist insanity. I stand there knowing that I have to tell barely 20-year-old's that race matters in all of the insane ways that they want to believe that it does not.

As a teacher, I stand on the boundary of subjectivity and objectivity. I am firmly planted in both places: my heart beats with a consciousness of my personhood and lived experiences inside of my black skin while I simultaneously aim to have my students hear the theories, narratives and evidence about the lives of Americans because of their race. "Just the facts, just tell them the facts," was my early shield. You know, the theories from immigration to stratification to racialization. If I could just get them to hear the histories and stories of northern and western Europeans, southern and eastern Europeans, Native Americans, Latin descent Americans, then maybe they would understand that race and the race problem was not equivalent to African ancestry, as I stand inside of my black skin.

Each time I stand there at the front of the room, I must come to terms with blackness as the racist reality and the escape hatch. It doesn't matter if it is the first day of the class or the last. It doesn't matter if the class is centered on the race lite of identity or the race heavy of American history. I feel and live the "problem" so expertly framed by DuBois. On the one hand, there is the assumption that I am equipped to address the subject because . . . you see . . . I am Black. There is also the other assumption – that I am, of course, angry

Teaching Race   65

about racism because of whom it is directed against and the existential fate of Black Americans. But what of the racism-laden histories of Native Americans, Southern and Eastern Europeans, Latin descent Americans, Asian descent Americans? I want to scream, "Have you not heard me!" "Did you do the readings!" Why lay this at the feet of Black Americans when racism is the history of the American Founding Fathers, you know, those White Anglo-Saxon Protestants? You know, the ones who have the intergenerational wealth from enslavement and the Industrial Revolution to ensure the invisibility of their privilege and the distribution of just enough "opportunity" to keep the rest of us deluded about racism. Just enough "opportunity" for the Horatio Alger novels to parade as the American reality.

If blackness is the escape hatch that protects all others who are not White Anglo-Saxon Protestants from racism, then Civil Rights legislation surely remedied the inequalities that resulted from the nation's origins in explicit and brutal racism. This is obviously so; I am at the front of the room. I am a Black, female, PhD. I am exactly the right age for Affirmative Action to open the doors of the academy for me. No need to consider my GPA or other academic credentials because surely the qualifier was my skin color. I mean, it is not as if the nation doesn't have a history of white skin color qualification. So, if Civil Rights legislation opened the doors, then the problem is solved. I mean, we moved from 1619 to the end of the Civil War in 1865, where African descent humans were the property of other (primarily) European descent humans. Next, we go from 1896 (Plessy v. Ferguson) to 1954 (Brown v. Board of Education) with legal race segregation that ensures race-based disadvantage for Americans of African descent (as well as others who were not racially white) and race-based opportunities and privileges for those of European descent. Then there is the Civil Rights Act of 1957, the Voting Rights Act of 1965 and the Civil Rights Act of 1968 and Affirmative Action Policy that addressed discrimination in employment, education and housing. Problem solved! Right? Done deal!

Across each semester, from the front of the room, I watch my students come to terms with disconcerting truths. From my point of view, black students settle into an acceptance that their skin color matters. This seems particularly hard for the children of recent African immigrants. This group and many of their African American peers are as middle/upper-middle class as their white classmates. It seems to be the same for Latin descent students; the truth that skin color is socially relevant is disconcerting. Yet, the group that seems to be hit the hardest are Asian descent students. It is as if they believed the hype of the model minority stereotype and were woefully ignorant of the history of race discrimination against Asian Americans. It seems that for many of the white students, the class is something of an endurance test, just something to get through. It isn't as if they are in denial about injustice, discrimination or oppression and their implications for what individuals experience. They seem to recognize the real-life consequences of systemic social inequalities. Yet, there are those occasions when I detect from them a sense of relief that their privilege is secure.

66   *Teaching Race*

I sincerely hope that my reader has detected the cynicism and sarcasm in what I have written. Framing the experiences of Americans of African descent as the problem of racism is to miss the point. The perpetrators of racism are the problem, not those that they target. More importantly, Black Americans are not the only targets of white racism. Yet if others who are not white are convinced that Blacks are fatally flawed and therefore rightfully disadvantaged, incarcerated and socially illegitimate, then to whatever degree their lives are better than those of (most) Black Americans, they are not the targets of racism. To whatever degree their lives are better than those of (most) Black Americans, then the cultural ideals of equality, opportunity, hard work and success are realities that they can strive for and achieve.

I am the Black girl at the front of the room whose dissertation chair could only give her a sideways "compliment" about her teaching skills, ensuring that it would also stick a knife in her back. Our common experiences of racial/racist realities, ranging from disadvantage to privilege, are the cornerstone of the United States and what makes each and every one of us American. As noted by DuBois, (white) America has offered the world so much. Americans of African descent have offered the world so much. This is also true of Americans who are not racially Black or white. My struggle in teaching the race lite of identity to the race heavy of American history is getting my students to see the reality of our nation. If racism is a Black thing, then it's a "personal problem." If racism is an American thing, then the human suffering that it causes should hang heavy on the hearts of all of us.

I am the person, the instructor, the teacher who must explain this to children. In explaining my sentiment, experience and reality in living up to that responsibility, I can only turn to the words of Marvin Gaye: "Oh, make you wanna holler/The way they do my life/Make me wanna holler/The way they do my life/This ain't livin', this ain't livin'/No, no baby, this ain't livin'/No, no, no."

Vaso

Teaching Toward Representation

My painful early life experiences, rooted in old-world ideas about girls and the American racism that infuriated my parents against my innocent Black boyfriend, spilled over into my school life as a young teacher. This cloud of emotionality made me feel connected to my students, as did our shared experiences as children of immigrants. We met there, in my early years of teaching, in our youth and in my careful instruction. We depart/ed at the color line; I am white; they are not. We depart in their inadvertent reminders that they have agency, minds of their own and unique communities of which they are a part. It is to this last departure that I have dedicated my teaching. It is this agency, rooted in an understanding of their own social conditions, that students embrace knowledge that transforms.

Teaching Race   67

First Memory

I was in my early twenties when I landed my first teaching job in NYC. The students were mostly African American, Puerto Rican and a few were Jamaican, Italian and Irish American. I didn't look much older than the students and didn't feel it either. I felt bonded with them as if my struggles were like their struggles, but I knew very little about them. I did know that they were poor; one had been homeless, another barely literate and quite a few in trouble with the law. Maybe the sadness of it all met mine. I struggled as a new teacher, and the students recognized it. I remember their laughter when I would nervously fumble with my misplaced notes, having lost my place in the developing lesson or when my exuberance for the lesson was far more than the topic warranted.

My tears came easily back then. I remember one day, I asked them to sit in a circle and read an article about the covert resistance of enslaved African women in the United States. My undergraduate readings still resonated with me then. It was a theoretical article, and we read it paragraph by paragraph, analyzing the vocabulary and ideas. After we finished our lesson in the circle, we began putting our chairs back into rows. I felt the tears well up in my eyes for my bad teaching, for me, of the enslaved women. I turned my back and started putting books away and wiping down the bookshelves. I remember one of my male students asking me, "What's wrong, 'Teach'? I know when women start cleaning, there's something bothering them." I wanted to cry but did not.

Bronx Community College

I came to the college classroom with a sense of connectedness to my students. Maybe it was all in my imagination. I thought that their minds would be blown away by the same content material that blew mine; after all, I came with a Marxist, feminist and anti-racist perspective to the classroom. I suspected this apathy when, for example, I assigned the first chapter of Patricia Hill Collins' *Black Feminist Thought*. As honors students, they read the article carefully and had ready feedback for me on the day we were to discuss the ideas. The inevitable "nature vs. nurture" argument began, the ole "is it the system or the individual?" that influences the lives of Black people, in this instance. One of my best students called out, "We do it to ourselves." I was confused; I meant to inspire, but the gravity of meritocracy and post-racialism did not escape this middle-class Caribbean girl. I wondered about how her class location shaped her perspective. We were departing in our understanding of the world.

Teaching Toward Representation and Multiple Identities

I always wanted my students to be heard, wanted their stories to be celebrated. I had to go beyond the standardized curriculum, beyond my assumptions about what might inspire them, and toward representing their communities and

68 *Teaching Race*

perspectives. Most of my students live in the local Dominican neighborhood of Washington Heights, some first-generation, others second-generation immigrants. Jamaican, Nigerian, Ghanaian, Bangladeshi and Guyanese immigrant students, as well as the children of earlier settlements of immigrant and racial groups to the area, such as Puerto Ricans and African Americans, also make up a significant part of the student body.

I've experienced student learning when they engage in a critical examination of their racial and ethnic communities. For example, they are exposed to the dynamic of the intersection of ethnicity, race and gender when we read and discuss Patricia Pessar's (1987) ethnography, "The Dominicans: Women in the Household and the Garment Industry." Dominican students have shared that their mothers' have worked in the informal sector of the NYC garment industry that the article addresses. They *are* the experts of their own communities and come to understand the personal is academic. Since they are connected to this experience, they are better able to think critically about the article and see their lives as worthy of scholarly reflection and study.

We read Nancy Foner's (1987) article, "The Jamaicans: Race and Ethnicity among Migrants in New York City," which raises questions about assimilation, race and class. The article reflects their NYC and Jamaican immigrant experiences and highlights the local Jamaican neighborhood on White Plains Road in the Bronx. This article points to the disparities between immigrants of African and European descent. The article demonstrates the role of race in the success patterns of racially diverse immigrant groups and challenges notions of race neutrality. The article departs from a cultural understanding of ethnic groups and claims, in essence, that race matters.

Joseph Healy's (2014) *Diversity and Society: Race, Ethnicity and Gender* and Vincent Parrillo's (2014) *Strangers to These Shores: Race and Ethnic Relations in the United States* provide a sociohistorical treatment of racial and ethnic groups in the United States. From my experience, a historical perspective provides the opportunity for students to explore the unique ways race, ethnicity, gender and the law explain the life chances and characteristics, otherwise perceived in stereotypical ways, of racial and ethnic groups. From a historical perspective, we can deconstruct the mythologies about different cultural and racial groups.

The inevitable connections and disconnections between the lived experiences of the students and the literature we read for the class raise questions and answers about marginality, identity and the history that underlies it. As students who are the first to attend college in their families, the exposure to ethnographies, articles and chapters that they can identify with, I believe, demystifies their experience and empowers them to shape new identities around being college students and, hopefully, progressive thinkers.

I focus on nuanced social locations in my instruction to illustrate the malleability of race and ethnicity and show how history and the racial structure shape these locations of inequality. For example, a short article written by a

Teaching Race 69

young Dominican woman from the Bronx, "I'm Not Black, I'm Dominican," resonates with my students as it addresses their complex identities as brown-skinned and ethnic (Castillo 2020). They read about how Julissa's identity as a Dominican girl in NYC was fundamentally based on her Dominican ethnicity and that her Africaness (the roots of Africa in the Caribbean) was not a part of how she saw herself. When she moved to Tennessee, still a young girl, her new community sought to categorize her as "mixed." She thought about the racial binary of Black and white; she thought about how she fit in. As a college student, she learned about her African roots and its political implications and she began to define herself as Afro-Latina. Julissa learned about *colorism*. We explore the issue of *colorism*, that is, the prejudice against individuals with a dark skin tone and African physical features. The students are keenly aware of colorism, in and out of their communities, in their families, on television and on social media. They share experiences of being called "negrita" (black girl) or "negrito" (black boy). We talk about the ideas of "pelo bueno" (good hair) and "pelo malo" (bad hair) and come to understand the gendered aspect of colorism. Teaching toward representation in a curriculum on race and ethnicity provides a space for students to feel empowered and motivated to learn as it builds on the familiar where students look for knowledge about their own communities.

As sociologists, we have always imparted a structural understanding to our students, certainly since the 1960s. In the current period of racial neoliberalism, however, this structural analysis of race and ethnicity has new and critical meaning. The cultural and contemporary belief that our society is multicultural yet equitable feeds into the compelling American and neoliberal notion that "we are all the same." This erases the painful experiences of racism for our Black and Brown students. This is not what we wanted when we moved away from a Eurocentric curriculum in my early years of teaching high school social studies. Then, we taught about the great ancient civilizations of Ghana and Mali, Mesopotamia and an African American history weaved into American history and American government. In this context, multiculturalism meant representing the unheard voices in a Eurocentric social studies curriculum. We didn't need a 1619 project then; we taught about African slavery and certainly started our unit on African American history with slavery. The inclusion of different experiences in the curriculum and social life was what multiculturalism meant to my fellow teachers and me then. All we wanted was for our students to see themselves reflected in the curriculum, to understand the world they live in, the one that has hurt them and to know that their lives matter.

Today, teaching and reading books about Black and Brown people are being banned around the country, framed as special treatment and even as racism against whites. This colorblind approach is actually racist. From my experience, helping students understand colorblind racism, that is, how denying that race matters, in the end, reproduces the very racism that a race-neutral society

70 *Teaching Race*

promises, is difficult. The idea of equality that racial neoliberal statements such as "I don't see color," "I am colorblind," "I see people, not color" and "We are all the same" evoke resonates powerfully and positively for my students and in a post-racial society. When I voice these quotes, my students are familiar with and agreeable to the notion of race neutrality, but when I ask them whether they thought the Minnesota police officer saw color when he fatally shot Philando Castile down after 40 seconds of encountering him, they become attentive and are closer to understanding how race neutrality is actually racist. Blackness, we agree, is essential to a truthful explanation of Castile's death.

I imagine my students perceive a great social distance between themselves and me as a white woman. Yet, I feel connected to them, if not by my shared experience as a child of immigrants or my over 30 years of teaching in NYC, then by my joy and sense of purpose when they show learning and the power of education in their lives.

Conclusion

As we carry our racialized selves into the classroom, we are not able to disassociate our experience outside of the classroom from the course content that we teach. Even if we could do so, teaching young adults that race identities are neutral identities, as racial neoliberalism would have us believe, would be impossible given the racialization and racism that informs the history and society of the United States. The inherent contradiction of being tasked with teaching about racism in a society or an institution and with a student body that often sees racism as a part of the past and less relevant in the present is difficult. While all instructors must work to teach their course material in ways that help students learn facts, skills, concepts and theories, we are tasked with the additional burden of persuading our students of a reality that they, and much of our larger society, including our higher education institutions, are often loathe to hear. We are tasked with telling our students that race does matter, that the system of white supremacy does exist and that their lives are significantly shaped by their skin color. We must do this at the same time as we ensure that our students are satisfied with their learning experience so that we keep our jobs and our academic reputations. And finally, we must do so as we wrestle with our own knowledge of the racial truths we are sharing and the experiences we have had with those truths.

References

Alexander, Michelle. 2019. *The New Jim Crow: Mass Incarceration in the Age of Color-blindness.* London: Penguin Books.

Alk, Howard, and Mike Gray. 1971. *The Murder of Fred Hampton.* Facets Multimedia Chicago Film Group, MGA Inc. Documentary.

Teaching Race 71

Bratt, Peter. 2017. *Dolores.* 5 Stick Films.

Breena, Clarke. 1999. *River, Cross My Heart.* Boston: Little, Brown and Co.

Brill, Marlene Targ. 2018. *Dolores Huerta Stands Strong: The Woman Who Demanded Justice.* Athens: Ohio University Press.

Brown, John. 1859. *Address of John Brown to the Virginia Court, When About to Receive the Sentence of Death, for His Heroic Attempt at Harper's Ferry to Give Deliverance to the Captives, and to Let the Oppressed Go Free . . . Boston.* Boston: Printed by C. C. Mead. www.loc.gov/item/rbpe.06500500/.

Bryan, Audrey. 2016. "The Sociology Classroom as a Pedagogical Site of Discomfort: Difficult Knowledge and the Emotional Dynamics of Teaching and Learning." *Irish Journal of Sociology* 24 (1): 10.

Castillo, Julissa. 2020. "I'm Not Black, I'm Dominican." *The Greanville Post*, December 15. www.greanvillepost.com/2020/12/15/im-not-black-im-dominican/.

Cazenave, Noel A. 2014. "Teaching About Systemic White Racism." In *Teaching Race and Anti-Racism in Contemporary America: Adding Context to Colorblindness*, edited by K. Haltinner, 249–56. New York, NY: Springer.

Chadwick, Justin. 2013. *Mandela: Long Walk to Freedom.* 20th Century Fox. Film.

Chavez, Dan D. 1996. *Soledad Chavez Chacon: A New Mexico Political Pioneer 1890–1936.* Albuquerque: University of Mexico Press.

Coates, Ta-Nehisi. 2015. *Between the World and Me.* 1st ed. New York, NY: Spiegel & Grau.

Collins, Patricia Hill. 2008. "Black Feminist Thought." In *Perspectives on Gender.* London: Routledge.

Davis, Angela Yvonne. 2021. *Angela Davis: An Autobiography.* Chicago: Haymarket Books.

DiAngelo, Robin J. 2018. *White Fragility: Why It's So Hard for White People to Talk About Racism.* Boston: Beacon Press.

Dretzin, Rachel, and Phil Bertelsen. 2020. *Who Killed Malcolm X?* Fusion. TV Series.

Duane, Kelly. 2019. *The Two Killings of Sam Cooke.* Netflix. Documentary.

DuBois, W. E. B. 1909. *John Brown, G.W.* Philadelphia: Jacobs and Company.

Du Bois, W.E.B. 1982. The Souls of Black Folk. *Signet Classic.* New York, NY.

DuVernay, Ava. 2014. *Selma.* 20th Century Fox. Film.

———. 2016. *13th.* Kandoo Films. Documentary.

Fleming, Crystal Marie. 2018. *How to Be Less Stupid About Race: On Racism, White Supremacy, and the Racial Divide.* Boston: Beacon Press.

Foner, Nancy. 1987. "The Jamaicans: Race and Ethnicity Among Migrants in New York City." In *New Immigrants in New York*, edited by Nancy Foner. New York, NY: Columbia University Press.

Freire, Paulo. 2000. *Pedagogy of the Oppressed.* New York, NY: Continuum.

Garbus, Liz. 2015. *What Happened, Miss Simone?* Netflix. Documentary.

Gaye, Marvin. 1971. "Inner City Blues/Make Me Wanna Holler." *What's Going on*, Tamia. Album.

Glaude, Eddie S. 2021. *Begin Again: James Baldwin's America and Its Urgent Lessons for Our Own.* New York, NY: Crown Publishing Group.

Haltinner, Kristin. 2014. "Conclusion: Lessons Learned – Pedagogical & Theoretical Strategies for Race." In *Teaching Race and Anti-Racism in Contemporary America: Adding Context to Colorblindness*, edited by K. Haltinner, 275–78. New York, NY: Springer.

72 *Teaching Race*

Harlow, Roxanna. 2003. "Race Doesn't Matter, But . . . : The Effect of Race on Professors' Experiences and Emotion Management in the Undergraduate College Classroom." *Social Psychology Quarterly* 66, no. 4 (December): 348.

Haynes, Todd. 2019. *Dark Waters.* Participant Productions. Film.

Healy, Joseph F. 2014. *Diversity and Society: Race, Ethnicity and Gender.* 4th ed. Los Angeles, CA: Sage Publications.

Indych-Lopez Anna. 2018. *Judith F. Baca.* Minneapolis: University of Minnesota Press.

Jenkins, Barry. 2016. *Moonlight.* A24 and Plan B Entertainment. Film.

Kaurismaki, Mika. 2011. *Mama Africa.* Millennium Films. Documentary.

Kim, Janine Young. 2016. "Racial Emotions of the Feeling of Equality." *University of Colorado Law Review* 87: 438–96.

Lee, Spike. 1982. *Malcolm X.* 40 Acres and a Mule Filmworks. Film.

Lee, Spike. 2001. *A Huey P. Newton Story.* 40 Acres and Mule Filmworks. Film.

Lemmons, Kasi. 2019. *Harriet.* Perfect World Pictures. Film.

Lerner, Gerda. 2004. *The Grimké Sisters from South Carolina: Pioneers for Women's Rights and Abolition.* Chapel Hill, NC: University of North Carolina Press.

Lewis, Avi. 2015. *This Changes Everything.* Louverture Films. Documentary.

Loewen, James W. 2018. *Lies My Teacher Told Me: Everything Your American History Textbook Got Wrong.* New York, NY: The New Press.

Luna, Diego. 2014. *Cesar Chavez.* Pantelion Films. Film.

Martin, Douglas. 2010. "Lolita Lebron, Puerto Rica Nationalist, Dies at 90." *New York Times,* August 3.

Matias, C. E., A. Henry, and C. Darland. 2017. "The Twin Tales of Whiteness: Exploring the Emotional Roller Coaster of Teaching and Learning About Whiteness Taboo." *The Journal of Culture and Education* 16 (1).

Morris, Monique W. 2016. *Pushout: The Criminalization of Black Girls in Schools.* New York, NY: The New Press.

Nelson, Stanley. 2015. *The Black Panthers: Vanguard of the Revolution.* 2015. Firelight Films. Documentary.

Norman, Matt. 2008. *Salute: The Story Behind the Image.* Wingman Pictures. Documentary.

Olmos, Edward James. 2006. *Walkout.* HBO. Film.

Olsson, Goran. 2011. *The Black Power Mixtape 1967–1975.* Louverture Films. Documentary.

Parrillo, Vincent N. 2014. *Strangers to These Shores: Race and Ethnic Relations in the United States.* 11th ed. New York, NY: Pearson Education.

Peck, Raoul. 2018. *The Young Karl Marx.* Agat Films and Cie. Film.

Pessar, Patricia. 1987. "The Dominicans: Women in the Household and the Garment Industry." *New Immigrants in New York,* edited by Nancy Foner. New York, NY: Columbia University Press.

Pittman, Chavella. 2010. "Race and Gender Oppression in the Classroom: The Experiences of Women Faculty of Color with White Male Students." *Teaching Sociology* 38 (3): 183–96.

Rae, Heather. 2005. *Trudell.* Independent Lens, PBS. Documentary.

Ritt, Martin. 1979. *Norma Rae.* 20th Century Fox. Film.

Sayles, John. 1987. *Matewan.* Cinecom Pictures. Film.

Schultz, Michael. 1983. *For Us, the Living: The Medgar Evers Story.* Charles Fries Productions. Film.

Sims, Bernice. 2014. *Detour Before Midnight: Freedom Summer Workers: James Chaney, Michael Schwerner, and Andrew Goodman Made an Unscheduled Stop*. La Verne: Lightning Source, Inc.

Sohn, Sonja. 2017. *Baltimore Rising*. HBO Films. Documentary.

Stevenson, Bryan. 2015. *Just Mercy: A Story of Justice and Redemption*. New York, NY: Spiegel & Grau.

Tuitt, Frank, Michele D. Hanna, Lisa M. Martinez, Maria Del Carmen Salazar, and Rachel Alicia Griffin. 2009. "NEA, Teaching in the Line of Fire: Faculty of Color in the Academy." *Thought and Action* (Fall): 65–74.

Washington, Harriet A. 2019. *Medical Apartheid*. New York, NY: Random House.

Zinn, Howard. 2015. *A People's History of the United States*. New York, NY: Harper Perennial.

3 Feeling Teaching Race

Introduction

When we enter our classrooms, we are conscious of our race identities and how they are framed socially and in academic literature. In other words, it is not possible to leave our knowledge and understanding of the social implications of race identities at the door. Moreover, our students know the assumptions and stereotypes that are associated with racial groups. While our primary goal as instructors is to expose them to the academic literature in this area, they enter the classroom with commonsense knowledge of the social implications of race and racism. However, what they don't want to know, yet we are charged with telling them, are the implications of race for them in terms of benefits and disadvantages. In the process, our courses challenge the common sense assumptions about racism: racism benefits those who are not its explicit targets, race groups that are characterized by social disadvantages are innately or culturally deficient, and, the converse, race groups that are economically and socially advantaged are in that position on the foundation of cultural and social values. The content of our classes disrupts these neoliberal assumptions.

It is in challenging assumptions, questioning cultural values and the legitimacy of socially accepted principles that teaching imparts learning in our students. It is here that the door of feeling teaching race is opened. It is here that the harms of racism are exposed. It is here that cultural values are revealed as nothing more than a mechanism for hiding the processes of systemic group-based social inequalities. It is here that the connections between race identities and the social processes that establish advantages and disadvantages are exposed, given the historical foundations and intergenerational transfers of valued social resources. Even if we teach our students that legislation has eliminated systemic social inequalities, we must also teach them that the inequalities of the past, present or future persist. This is the emotional experience of teaching Race Studies courses: we must tell them the history of what has happened, and in doing so, we reveal that it is still happening. It is this revelation that strikes us at our core as we reveal to another classroom of young adults that race does matter.

DOI: 10.4324/9781003442448-4

Adriana

I grew up Brown and female in Amherst in the 1970s with activist parents, revolutionaries, students, and educators committed to social protest and a new society. I also lived in India twice before the age of ten, and in 1980 we moved to Wilmington, Delaware, a small city heavily segregated along race and class lines. After high school, I went to college and entered, for the first time in my life, an abyss of whiteness. Although all of my friends at college were people of color, UD was a Primarily White Institution (PWI), and there I became scared of whiteness.

When I teach, I bring all of my past experiences into the classroom. This includes my knowledge of myself as a woman of color and the passion, energy, excitement and commitment to social justice that grounded my early years in Amherst, as well as the horrors of racism in Wilmington. In the classroom, I am a woman of color performing: I juggle warring emotions and try not to fall off the tightrope. In this chapter, I discuss what it feels like to teach about race and racism in a body marked by otherness.

Unmasked

My fear of public speaking developed at UD and solidified as I worked on my MA. It followed me to Temple University (TU), where I started to work on my Sociology PhD in the Fall of 1995. After a two-year research assistantship, I was awarded a teaching assistantship. For the first two to three years of the teaching assistantship, I sat through lectures, took notes, graded papers, tutored students and held office hours. I was eventually assigned my own class – a night section of an Introduction to Sociology course. I was terrified. I was not scared to teach because I was unprepared. In fact, "preparedness" was my armor. My mother told me from an early age that as a girl of color, I would always have to do double the work to get half the credit as any white man.

I took her advice to heart; I worked extra hard and was usually over-prepared. I never wanted to look like I did not know what I was doing. I researched all of my topics well in advance, fully wrote out entire lectures and even practiced what I was going to say repeatedly so that I knew what I was going to say well before I actually said it. I still do the same thing to this day. Nonetheless, when I teach about race and racism, I know my voice is going to shake, and I hate it. The root of my trembling voice stems from the fact that at UD, I became scared to challenge injustice in classes full of predominantly white students because I knew I would be attacked, delegitimized and denied. This did not stop me from speaking up, but my voice made me look unsure and as if I lacked confidence. My shaky voice conveys that I am unsure, incompetent, unprepared.

I remember how frightened I was to teach that night class! I knew my voice would betray me. I remember that my voice shook during the

76 *Feeling Teaching Race*

entire three hour-long class, that my stomach hurt and that after the class was over, I did indeed get sick. I also remember a light-skinned Jamaican woman in the class who sat in the front and paid attention to every word I uttered. I remember being embarrassed by my voice for both me and her. That first class is unforgettable. The memory of it is always right there, reminding me of my fear.

After that class, I taught another course at Temple University Center City (TUCC) titled American Ethnicity. I remember a burly young white guy who sat to the left of me in the front of the class. He had reddish brown hair, and although he didn't seem angry or obnoxious, he always asked a million questions and made plenty of remarks. He told me I didn't say words correctly and that I pronounced the textbook author's name incorrectly. I recall my stomach hurting every time I saw him, yet I always acted happy to see him, even though he made me miserable.

The Mask

I started working full-time (tenure track position) at Delaware County Community College (DCCC) in September 2001. At the start of my teaching career, I found myself becoming increasingly frustrated with my students because I felt unable to reach many of them. Some refused to acknowledge that racism existed, and others refused to "accept" or "believe" that macro-level factors shaped and impacted group behavior and dynamics. I felt my role was to convince students to see the reality of racism and understand the power of structures on group behavior. In the classroom, I felt like I was failing in this endeavor.

My feelings of inadequacy were complicated because students usually did not outright challenge the content in my classes. They often challenged me in very passive-aggressive ways, such as refusing to pay attention in class. They talked while I was lecturing. They played with their electronic devices. They passed notes at times. They went to sleep. They came late and left early. These passive-aggressive behaviors left me unsettled and angry.

I believe the power struggles I experienced were about race-based course content mixed with my femaleness, even if they were masked as something else. Students are often required to take my class, and many enter the course apprehensive about the material. They definitely do not want to hear about white privilege/fragility, white violence and racist public/social policy from a 5'3" woman of color, so there is push back early, creating tension in the classroom from the start.

One day I was lecturing about the intersection of race and class, and a white student raised her hand and commented that people were poor because they were lazy and did not work hard. She continued – insinuating but not explicitly stating – that if Black Americans were poorer than other groups, it was because they would rather be on welfare than work. I had the data to destroy

Feeling Teaching Race 77

her point, and I shared research with the class to illustrate this. I knew I had "won" content-wise but my voice shook when I talked, and I knew I did not sound confident. After I was done talking, she said, "You work at a community college, what do you know about anything?" Although it was posed as a question, it was a statement, and she was not looking for a response. I was appalled by the blatant disrespect, but instead of showing my pain, I laughed and made some sort of joke (which probably was not very funny). I remember the hurt and embarrassment I felt because I was put down by a student in front of the entire class – not for doing anything wrong, making a mistake or treating someone unfairly – but merely for teaching something she had no desire to hear. As I sit and write, I still remember her face, her hair, the classroom and her name, 15 years later.

A few years later, I was teaching a 12:10–1:35 PM Introduction to Sociology class to 30 students in the basement of our academic building. The classroom was small, and I liked it. There were no windows, and I felt like I was in a cocoon-like bomb shelter tucked away from the noise and commotion of the main hallways. I had a white male student in the class who was 6+ feet tall, skinny, blonde, and had blue eyes and wore glasses. He used to come to class straight from work, so he was usually dressed in khakis and a button-down shirt. He was not particularly interested in me or the class, but he needed the course for his work-related continuing education credits. He pretended to be pleasant and polite, but I quickly sensed resentment and anger seething closely beneath the surface. He was a ticking time bomb, waiting to explode on me and my lectures.

As we moved into the material on race and racism, he began to get testy, constantly challenging me and asking question after question after question. I quickly realized that he was more interested in a physical response from me than a factual or data-driven one. He asked questions to unnerve me, all the while smiling politely. He was passive-aggressive, and was hell-bent on making me sweat. One day in class, I was being evaluated by a peer and I said something about Southeast Asian countries, and he proceeded to ask me to list them all. I responded with a joke and a smile and moved on to the next topic as I felt the heat rise on my back and sweat run down my spine.

A few days later, he began to ask questions about stereotypes, and I could see that he was angry. He informed the class that there were many more stereotypes about whites than Blacks. I let him talk. I was more quiet than usual as I leaned against the wall in front of his first-row seat on the left side of the room. I remember hating him and wanting him to shut up. He then offered that he was angry about the stereotype that white men have smaller penises than Black men. The primarily white class turned to collectively look at him – there was a collective "OH MY" etched on their surprised (white) faces. He then proceeded to ask me where the stereotype came from, and then without waiting for an answer (thank you, Lord!), informed the class that it was a racist stereotype. He became angrier and angrier and lost his composure. I remained

78 *Feeling Teaching Race*

stock still and watched him unravel around the edges. I remember the flush in my body as he spoke, the heat on my back and neck. I remember not wanting to engage him in this sexual conversation as he told the class he did not have a small penis. Not sure what to do with 30 students watching us, I moved on. I remember many things, but I still can't remember how I responded verbally that day. I tried to de-escalate. I remember my hands shaking as the other students looked at him like a weirdo.

Teaching is tricky; there is always a balancing act that takes place, and as much as I was – and am – convinced that my content is usually outstanding, the actual act of performing and presenting that content to an audience that is not convinced that you are right, or smart, or valuable or important, is daunting.

My increasing frustration with my students was apparent in various ways at that time. Sometimes my exasperated facial expressions gave me away. Sometimes I would debate and argue with students after the time to stop had passed. Sometimes I spoke with an agitated tone. I remember the time I decided to teach them about a number of racist laws rapid-fire, so they would be forced to acknowledge that racism was real. I knew this content overwhelmed them, and I was glad it did. I believe showing my emotions decreased student engagement because I was, at times, upset and frustrated when I taught. Nonetheless, I realized my increasing anger – due to white student denial of the existence of racism – did not help facilitate a successful pedagogy. It merely made students uncomfortable and less likely to engage. Showing my anger also resulted in students stereotyping me as the "angry woman of color."

I have always brought all my feelings into the classroom. In fact, my feelings are an invisible entourage keeping me company. In time, however, I had to figure out how to untangle my multiple tensions and perform as if my feelings did not exist in order to teach successfully. I had to split my personality into compartments and don a mask to camouflage the pain of teaching about racism. This is one way in which teaching about race and racism is different from teaching other courses. I had to learn how to act as if content that is disturbingly violent and terrifying is not. I had to disassociate in order to survive. This, though, made me feel like I was teaching from a lie.

In order to teach about race and racism successfully (whatever that means), I must appear calm and at ease even though underneath this, I am outraged, I am angry, I am in pain. Although my emotions in the classroom constantly fluctuate, I must hide them. This is an exhausting process and requires emotional labor, self-control and stamina.

I learned to don a mask in order to survive my students. When I teach, I appear upbeat, full of energy and smiles. But how can anyone teach about racism and be value-neutral and unaffected? As a woman of color raising Black children in White America, this is an impossible task, one which I will constantly fail, regardless of how hard I try. Although I am often able to mask my

Feeling Teaching Race 79

face, I am unable to mask my voice. As hard as I try to hide my feelings, I have never learned how to tame my voice. It signifies that I am in trouble, that America has failed us. My voice reveals that we are not safe.

The mask analogy is drawn from DuBois's idea of double consciousness in *Souls of Black Folk* (2008); Paul Lawrence Dunbar's poem *We Wear the Mask* (1913); Fanon's discussion in *Black Skin White Masks* (1952) about the mask colonized people must don to survive colonialism; and Marc Black's (2007) timely conversation on the mental turmoil associated with attempting to survive a dual identity. When I discuss the mask I wear in the classroom, I am referring to the mental as well as physical and emotional conflict I experience when I teach about race and racism.

Along with masking my facial emotions when I teach, I also now enter the classroom with emotional body armor. I place a physical barrier between my students and myself. When I teach, I tell my students that I am going to share information with them that they are going to have to learn, apply and write about, but that I do not care about their opinions or reactions to the material. I tell them this in a matter-of-fact tone because I have learned to protect myself from student reactions and opinions – that is, their harsh words and dismissiveness. I have been left to save myself.

I tell them I do not teach an "opinions-based" course, and I clearly state this in my syllabus. If they decide to embrace the material, I appreciate it, but if they choose to resist the information and not believe it, that is their prerogative. I clearly state, at the start of the semester and in my syllabus, that regardless of their approach to the material, in order for them to be successful in the class, they will still have to read the material, understand it, discuss it and write about it. They will have to pass the tests whether they like, accept or believe the material. In the past, I would get upset if students challenged the material or refused to accept that racism exists.

Conclusion

Although teaching about race and racism as a woman of color is fraught with land mines, teaching is simultaneously a way to fight back and a road toward liberation. Without historical knowledge and sociological imagination, we cannot work to reenvision society. When I teach about race and racism and macro-level systems, my aim is to move us forward as a collective. In the classroom, I am motivated by acts of resistance and revolution, and I am often in a very positive head-space, one in which there is always a strong sense of community, belonging and a shared idea of collective responsibility to make our social systems more just. Wedding teaching and learning to activism – and thus optimism – is a goal I have not only for myself but for all of my students as well.

80 *Feeling Teaching Race*

Donna-Marie

In Elizabethan England, rural audiences attending plays by William Shakespeare were peasants, called groundlings. They had a reputation for expressing their displeasure with disappointing productions by standing for hours throwing rotten tomatoes at actors while they performed. At times, they joined the actors on stage, comically making fun of them to the amusement of the audiences. In the early days of teaching, the push-back that I received from individuals deflected the focus away from me to them. It was the onset of a mental health breakdown that caused a student of color to bring the class to a sudden halt.

Exploding Minefield

AUTHORITY, AUTHORITY, AUTHORITY is the word rapidly pounding repeatedly in my ear – I can't understand what this attractive strongly-built Black female student, older than others in the class, is angrily saying to them. She is escalating. "Class is dismissed," I announce, attempting to de-escalate. As students hurry towards the door, she begins to confront me and I suddenly realize that I am the subject of her ire. She screams, "**You** think you have authority over me! **You** are not my authority! You have too much authority! **You** don't have authority over me!"

Before that moment, I hadn't considered myself the authority figure in the classroom. I avow egalitarian values in my classroom and stress independent thinking.

> *I'm not your mother.*
> *I'm not your father.*
> *I'm not your sister.*
> *I'm not your brother.*
> *I'm your teacher.*

This is the rap that I say to myself as a reminder to maintain a cool distance from my student, which is contrastingly different from everyday familial relations. I could be this student's mother, her aunt, her grandmother. She could be my daughter, my niece or my second cousin. Although I keep my emotions hidden when I teach to maintain an air of objectivity, my exterior begins to crack. "I'm Black, she's Black," you say to yourself. "How can I be the enemy?" Hostility from someone of my own race is painful, almost too much to bear. I feel myself having an out-of-body experience as I step outside my well-practiced, reserved demeanor – a well-worn, protective armor. I say to this out-of-control, hysterical student, "You don't know what I go through in class struggling to teach students, many of whom consider me a racist just for teaching the subject of race." I try to fight back my tears. I am extremely embarrassed to find

Feeling Teaching Race 81

myself showing emotions in front of my student. At this moment, together, we are experiencing a bout of racial trauma. My tears bring the verbal attack against me to an immediate halt and my student begins apologizing profusely. "I didn't know, I didn't know this is what you go through," she says, watching me wipe away my tears. A few seconds tick away; she becomes overly protective. With an air of confidence, she says, "Don't worry Dr. Peters, I got your back!" United by the mounting pain faculty inflict upon her, and students inflict upon me, I say, "And I got yours."

Although you are committed to helping students maintain their dignity, it is from this experience that you begin to wonder if they see your humanity. There are no quid-pro-quo reciprocity agreements between student and teacher. You think about the vicious comments that they make about you on their student evaluations. As soon as you appear in front of the class on the first day of the semester, you feel students responding in different ways to your skin color. One semester, a female student refused to wait until she spent a few weeks in class before labeling me a racist. She was only in class for one and a half hours. In an email, she cryptically wrote to me, "You are a racist, and my friends think so too! I'm dropping your class!" You go over in your head all that you did on the first day of class. You wonder if going over your syllabus and having the students introduce themselves by participating in an icebreaker could be interpreted as demonstrating racism. I would spend the entire semester feeling intimidated by my students – overly scrutinizing daily lectures and reluctant to discuss the more controversial, contemporary race-related topics of the day. I could feel the askance glances by the students who considered me to be a racist – that happened behind my back. I was a prisoner in my own classroom. There was no way to confront my accusers.

Your thoughts turn to the international adjunct professor from India with whom you spoke one semester. He wasn't afraid to show his vulnerability to students. He explains to you how he bravely confessed to them that he lacked knowledge about race in America. He hadn't studied the subject matter at his university in India or experienced racism in America as a newcomer to this country. He explained to me that his students empathized with him and, furthermore, came to his rescue. The students became the teachers, and everyone's knowledge about race deepened.

Students looked at him and saw humanity, you realize. You want students to see you in this way and not "that Black female in front of the room who has to grade me." You try augmenting your teaching repertoire. "I am a relic of history," you say embarrassingly. "How can facts be false if I experienced it?" You then begin to teach the pain you experienced as a child to better explain de facto segregation in the North. You don't hide your feelings. You tell your students about the lived experience of desegregating a white suburban town in the north. You describe three fires set by racists in front of your house that caused you to have a lifelong fear of fire. A student says, "I feel you." That day, I finally felt humanized.

82   *Feeling Teaching Race*

The Minefield: The Boys in the Back of the Room

Like Klansmen who came home from hangings to hug their wives and kiss their children, students can be deeply duplicitous. There are seemingly, sincerely smiling students silently sitting in wait to find the opportune time behind your back to unexpectedly tie a noose around your neck to frighten and silence you.

After the first month of teaching, the worldview of students begins to change, and student resistance lessens. The classroom that was once a battlefield has now become a minefield; you traverse issues fluidly but cautiously. You go for weeks without facing student wrath. You become more comfortable teaching students and gradually begin to choose your words with less apprehension. You fool yourself that there are no residual effects of battle. You come to believe that every student in your large classroom has experienced cognitive change and awareness. But, still, there are days when you accidentally step on a sensitive topic that causes tempers to detonate without warning, like a hidden bomb in a minefield.

The first day of each semester, you psychologically reserve back-row seats for them to occupy throughout the semester. From years of experience, their class enrollment is anticipated. They are the white boys in the back of the room who are the habitual albatross around your neck. Most days, you try to ignore them. At first, when you look at them, they offer a smile. They think you can't see their faces as they spend much of the class period hunched over, whispering in each other's ears and laughing. You feel that they are laughing at you. When you look directly at them once again, in an effort to stop their antics, they pay you no mind and continue their behavior, taunting, daring you to call them out. But you don't.

Your singleness of purpose keeps you laboring to change minds, then hearts, of often-reluctant students. You sit in your office anxiously seeking evidence of student learning. You are reading voices of self-discovery in the handwritten short reflection papers that they recently submitted. You are pleased that the in-class activity that they performed opened their eyes to the lack of real diversity in their lives outside of classroom diversity. You feel pleased that your students trust you enough to be honest in their self-reflections. "They are beginning to get it," you say to yourself. Your thoughts momentarily turn to how surprised you are that the stubborn tulips in your front garden are blossoming. You pat yourself on the back and say to yourself, "Another step forward in achieving changed cognitive awareness in students!" Then, you receive a reflection paper in illustrated form: a rough, crudely-drawn picture of ejaculating male genitalia – cowardly, unsigned and drawn to evoke shock and pain.

The next day, you try to ignore the two white boys in the back of the room as you begin the class. But you can't keep your eyes off them. You know who your assailants are: the two white boys on the right side of the class, in the first two seats of the last row. The fires of your youth still burn in your subconscious as the smug look on their faces paralyzes you speechless.

Feeling Teaching Race   83

Like many female victims of sexual assault, there is no closure. Sexual assault is about power and control. You can no longer keep the drawing to yourself. With the passage of each classroom day, you feel yourself sinking into psychological death. It's been a month of classes – teaching without a modicum of closure. The anger is now boiling over inside of you. With your secret folded inside your handbag, you march down the hall to the office of the sociology department and, without an appointment, demand to see the male department chair.

You slap the symbol of white male supremacy that hangs like a noose around your neck onto his desk. At first, you see horror in his eyes and then a sadness that overwhelms him. He is silent; you are silent. At last, the atrocity behind the secret I was keeping has been witnessed. We commune in silence – exorcizing away from my spirit the negative power of a simple drawing. Uplifted, I walk out the door after he makes me promise to throw into the trash this illustrative document of the perils of teaching. But certain traumas aren't forgotten.

Leaving the Field: Last Class

No longer a minefield, your classroom has become a field of active discovery and transformational learning as designed. It is the last day of class. One video at a time, each group pulls up on the screen their newly created public service announcements for all to see. Students were asked to, as a group, write, film (with their cell phones) and edit a public service announcement that attempts to convince a specific audience that diversity is important. One group produces a public service announcement that is modeled toward convincing students their age to attend our university. The video ends with the tagline: *Great Minds Think Differently, Diversity Matters Here, Our Differences Bring Us Together*!

You gaze at the clock. You suddenly realize that you are running out of time. But there is so much more you need to discuss about the importance of diversity and empathy toward others. You think about how in the black church, the preacher brings his sermons to a crescendo as he perspires and wipes his brow. Congregants respond to his message with Amens and shouts – someone may even faint or begin speaking in tongues as they feel the spirit. You wish your classes could elicit a similar impact. Finality brings you pause, and you have a self-revelatory moment:

I teach because I am happy.
I teach because I am sad.
I teach because you will leave me soon.
I teach because I once was the only one in the room.

With an acute sense of ending, you bring the class to a close. "I grew up in a world without diversity," I say to my students as they begin to pack up to leave.

84 *Feeling Teaching Race*

"Diversity is the heart of why I teach race. The classroom," I continue, "is one place where no one should be left alone like I was!"

Mary

After more than 20 years of teaching Race Studies classes, I feel as if I finally have a plan, a plan to empower my students to join the struggle for racial justice through a carefully crafted education on the history and significance of race in the United States. This feels good. But it often feels that if I make one false move, I will lose them and my plan will be destroyed. If I reveal too early on, for example, that they must act, they will get frightened by the prospect and shut down. Or if they feel *too* implicated *too* early, they will rebel and cling to the status quo that has offered them some level of comfort. Thus I always feel nervous, trying to slowly and carefully lead them to these understandings on their own. I am always afraid that this won't happen, that my plan will fall short, and of course, for the most part, it does. And yet even though I know my plan will fall short again and again, I continue to fear this most likely outcome because when the plan doesn't work, my ego suffers and I feel a great level of insecurity about who I am and what I'm doing. When students remain indifferent, feel too overwhelmed by their lives to engage in the struggle or feel too sad, angry or defensive, I feel as if I have failed, failed as a "good white person" and failed as an instructor. Of course, this is exactly what critical pedagogue Paulo Friere (2000) warns against, this arrogant notion that we can change the world with one course, but it is a difficult notion for me to shake, and it informs what I am feeling when I am teaching Race Studies courses, that inner story, those most personal thoughts that will explain what it feels like for me in the classroom over the course of a semester.

Me, Day 1 Inner Story

Deep breath. Just breathe, STAY CALM. Be kind. Be likable. Build rapport. Don't Blink. Don't sugarcoat. Okay, class isn't as white as I thought it was so that's good. Deep breath. Break the ice. Made it, phew, one down. So far to go.

Me, Day 2 Inner Story

Here we go. Deeper breath. Stay calm. Be kind. Be likable. Build rapport. Don't blink. Don't sugarcoat. Signal carefully where I stand. Oh, Liz is with me – thank god. John is distancing. I need to keep an eye on that one. He's going to be a problem. Shit. Two down. So far to go.

Me, Day 3 Inner Story

Breathe in, Breathe out. Don't look at John. No, wait, smile at John. No, wait, just breathe. Stop worrying about John. But why is he smiling with that kid next

Feeling Teaching Race 85

to him? Damnit, I hate this. I'm sure they are mocking me. Why am I doing this? I'm a grown woman worrying about these arrogant little . . . What else could I do at this point to make money? Oh, stop it, you're so dramatic. For god's sake, you have a great life; check your fucking privilege. Three down. I can do this. I really don't know if I want to anymore.

Me, Day 4 Inner Story

Let's see if they got it. Listen to them. Wow, I didn't realize Scarlett was with me. Did John just say white supremacy is the problem? That it didn't have to be this way? He did. He did. Okay, I'm doing this. But Rana – she doesn't look okay. Shit. It's too much. This is all too much. I shouldn't be subjecting Black kids to all of this. Lighten the mood. Reach out. Deep breath. Maybe just a little sugarcoat. Pause on the horror. Highlight resistance. Next class. I can do this.

Me, Day 5 Inner Story

Okay, focus, focus. Deep breath. Rana is absent. Shit. It was too much. Breathe.

"They fought back. They loved. They laughed. They fought back. They exist outside of white supremacy!"

Okay, good, good, but don't lose sight of the horror. Be careful not to romanticize the resistance. Because really, they were not okay. But don't remind them today. Rana is absent. Damn.

Me, Day 6 Inner Story

Rana is back. With a doctor's note. She was sick. Probably why she didn't look okay. SMDH. Seriously, I need to get over myself. I really don't even know if they are reading or listening. This is my job. They love. They laugh. They exist outside of my class. Lighten up, Mary. Wait, is "lighten up" a racist phrase? Oh my god, listen to myself. But I need to look that up.

Me, Day 12 Inner Story

Okay, so I fucked up last time. My bright red ears and booming voice betrayed me. But you have to stop triggering me with that meritocracy crap! I just went over this!

"Have you ever considered that you might be underqualified? That you might have messed up the interview, and that's why you didn't get the damn job? Have you ever considered that that Black guy might just be better than you?"

*Okay, they saw my anger, but I can bring it back. Be nice. Re-build rapport. Why in the fuck did I have to say that to him? Did 12 years of meditation teach me nothing? **Don't be defensive**. Do NOT attack him. Do NOT. Jesus, how many times do I have to remind myself? This isn't how to reach them. You have*

86 *Feeling Teaching Race*

to like him. Call him in – not out. Be nice. Re-build rapport. Remember those evaluations – shit.

Me, Day 22 Inner Story

Okay, let's do this. Just do it. You know they don't want to hear this. It's okay. You don't need to fear it. Remember? Just be aware. Stay in the moment. Just let it come. Stay calm. Respond calmly. Tell them. Now tell them again where you stand. Tell John. Look at him. Carefully. Calmly. But tell them. Tell John. Tell Rana. Tell Scarlett. Tell Liz. Tell them all. I think I can reach all of them. I think I have reached all of them. I'm really good at this. I'm a good white person. I'm a good instructor. Wait . . . what did he just say? Shit.

Me, Last Day of Class, Inner Story

I really didn't spend enough time on affirmative action. They didn't seem to get the urgency of reparations. Did I forget to show them that immigration video? I'm going to be more organized next semester. I'm going to cover all of it. Christ. Just breathe. I did my best. That's all I can do. I'm doing "the work." Miss Martin would be proud of me.

Conclusion

Teaching Race Studies classes makes me feel scared, beaten down and yet also very powerful and even hopeful. I feel scared because I know that what I am teaching will be met with anger, resentment and even mockery from more than a few students, most of them white, and it's always scary to deal with those emotions/behaviors, particularly when I am charged with being their instructor. And I feel scared because the material hurts students deeply, most of them of color, and it pains me to see the pain in their faces and bodies, and I'm scared of feeling and seeing this. And I feel scared because I know that what *I* feel about race is a lot of anger and resentment, and I don't want to let that anger and resentment prevent me from getting students to hear what I am telling them, but without fail, every semester, at some point, my anger is unleashed. When these moments happen, I feel beaten down and disappointed in myself and in the world that makes me feel such anger. And I also feel beaten down because while my pedagogical "plan" is solid, I know what Friere says is true – no matter how great my plan – it's just a class. And yet I can't stop myself from hoping that I will be able to move mountains. I can't help but feel powerful when I am telling them the truths that nobody has told them before. I can't help but feel powerful when they sit up straight to hear me better and begin nodding their heads. When they see it. When they feel it. Just like I do. For at least a moment. I feel hopeful, then. I take this with me, all of it, when that first day comes, as it inevitably does. *Deep Breath.*

Michelle

In what follows, I provide four brief glimpses into my experiences of teaching undergraduates about the societal importance of racism as it organizes human experiences in the United States. These snapshots move across my professional career as an academic and sociologist, beginning with my teaching experiences as a graduate student. The stories are brief, yet they expose my consciousness of the importance of having my students understand that racism and the quality of human suffering that it creates in our society is not an accit.

4. 1. *The Black Girl at the Front of the Room*

I am at the front of the classroom, looking out at students who are mostly white and someplace between solidly middle and upper class. There are a few Black students in the room, maybe four or so. They are seated in the front two rows near the door. I can see them out of the side of my eyes, but I am not really looking at them. It's a science classroom, with one of those long unmovable stone-top podium-like tables, with brown wooden drawers and cabinets and a sink with a curved faucet that is off to my left. The door to the classroom is to my left, too, as are the Black students. On my right are long paned windows that flood the room with sunlight. The students are seated at long tables, facing me. My throat is tight. I don't know how I am going to speak. I want to cry, but I know that I cannot. I have made a huge mistake: I have asked them to read slave narratives for today's class for our discussion. And the sorrow of it is washing over me. I have lectured about this part of our nation's history, an appropriate topic for a course titled The Black Community. I added the narratives to the reading list in hopes of making the history of Americans of African descent more "real"; in hopes of having them understand something of the "living of blackness." What I did not anticipate was my own pain in having to talk about, to acknowledge the voices of the enslaved in front of this room of young, privileged white children. I open the discussion, forcing myself to speak, to review the content of the readings. I know the Black students are watching me; I train my gaze to the middle of the room, trying not to look at anyone in particular. Eventually, I come to my favorite question, "What do you think?" or its close cousin, "What do you remember from the reading?" The room is silent – I know that I must have tried to fill it with some detail from the reading and another question, "What impressed you or what did you learn from this that you did not know?" A white female student raises her hand. I call on her. She says, "You seem angry." I know she said more, but I can't remember. Other students – at least three, male and female, all white – speak in support of her evaluation of me. I am back to wanting to cry and amazed that they are reading my sorrow as anger. I eventually find my voice and explain that what they are reading as anger is intense sorrow. The Black students come alive; they support me and the pain of having read the voice of suffering among the enslaved.

88 *Feeling Teaching Race*

2. *Race and the Urban University*

It is one of my early years at TU. It is still an urban university. In other words, it had not yet become an urban "destination" university. The difference is significant. The urban university served the city's population. The students were drawn from the various neighborhoods of the city. The poor, the working-class, the middle-class, the white ethnic identified, the Black, the Latino and Asian, mostly first-generation students but many whose parents had attended college. The "destination university" is different: it is more white, more middle and upper middle class, more engaged in the "college experience" than as a ticket to social-class mobility. The class was American Ethnicity. The race lite, ethnic incorporated, diversity-focused version of my class in race and racism. The agenda: the telling of histories, opportunity structures and discriminations as they manifested themselves across the race/ethnic groups of Americans. The class had a particular resonance for the students of the "urban university" because somewhere in there, the story of their community, neighborhood and identity was told. Moreover, for me, the implied (but rarely explicit) comparative lens allowed the students to understand race-based hierarchies and inequalities without the use of the blunt instrument of explicitly acknowledging racism – although everyone knew that it was there. In this particular semester, a group of Black students, mostly female, had positioned themselves in the seats in front of my desk. Other Black students were scattered throughout the room. The overwhelming majority of the students were white, but TU is a diverse university, so there were Asian and Latin descent students too. Just behind that cluster of about five Black girls who sat at the front of two rows was a white guy. He had grown up in one of the white ethnic neighborhoods of the city. The class began by outlining the origins of the nation, that is, the incursion of western and northern Europeans into the territory of the Native Americans. Again, the agenda was the telling of both sides of this history and its societal implications for the groups involved and the nation. It, of course, marked the significance of the population of African descent in the founding of the nation, but the more contemporary social circumstance of the community would be covered later in the semester. First, we had to visit the migration of southern and eastern European ethnic groups to the US, outlining both the history of discrimination and the opportunity structures that defined the group's Americanization. It seems that this history of explicit discrimination within the boundaries of whiteness is glossed over and minimized, if not totally ignored, in the telling of white race and American history. That white guy from the white ethnic corners of Philly came alive. He finally heard the story, the telling of the history of his family, his neighborhood and the NOT middle-class existence of his life. He got it, the reason why! And then, we returned to blackness – remembering but not belaboring the story of the enslaved as we covered the causes and consequences of anti-Black discrimination. But he was not having it; that white guy who finally knew something of the social consequences of white

Feeling Teaching Race 89

ethnicity was not about to stand for the framing of discrimination as a plight of blackness. There was no need, from his point of view, to acknowledge its salience and persistence in framing the Black American experience. There was no need to believe that there was something unique, unbearable and persistent in the Black experience of social exclusion when – as covered in the prior weeks – white "ethnics" had experienced discrimination too. He took on the debate at every word challenging me and the cause of any uniqueness of racism with regard to being of African descent. But the Black girls, that cluster in front of my desk, and other Black students just were not having it. The room would erupt in heart-felt debates. As our conversations of histories moved forward and the cases of Asians and Latino came to the fore, the wildness of it all expanded and continued pulling other students into the discussions of the internment and exclusions of those of Asian descent, the land theft and second-class citizenship of those of Latin descent. It was fun; they were engaged; they were learning and dealing with what they had not known about the United States and the histories of groups of Americans. But that white guy, he seemed enraged at me; he challenged his peers, and they challenged him back. I was absolutely certain that he harbored some special anger at me for exposing all of this, some disgust that occasionally burst forth in the expression on his face. And then, one day, I was at the mall not far from my home. My daughters, elementary school-aged, and I were in Macy's. I was buying a new set of pots and pans. I walked up to the counter to pay for my purchase, and there he stood; that white guy from my American Ethnicity class. The shock at seeing me – and my daughters – registered on his face. I was surprised too, and I am sure that it showed. I am not certain, but it is very likely that I introduced him to my daughters. Something changed at that moment, but I was not sure of what. As the semester continued, he was calmer in class, more relaxed, not quite angry anymore. I decided that in that chance meeting, finally, he saw me as a person, just another human being, as more than the "blackness" of my skin.

3. Teaching "Race" in the Lecture Hall

The class was titled, The History and Significance of Race in America. It was the new and updated version of Race and Racism. I sat on the committee that designed the course as a part of the general education curriculum. In truth, I preferred the course on Race and Racism. It had allowed me to teach the various sociological theories of race and ethnic relations. To point out their logic and their applicability in the analysis of race and ethnic-based social inequalities. Moreover, the Race and Racism course had given me the platform to teach students about the constitutional logic and Supreme Court cases that legitimated the racial segregation and the inequalities of Jim Crow America as well as the legislative agenda that was established by the Civil Rights Movement and the anti-discrimination legislation that rested on the Constitutional

90 *Feeling Teaching Race*

principle of the "specific intent to discriminate." But, this new course asked for something different; it asked for the telling of our history of race and its social relevance with potentially only the briefest of acknowledgments, if that, to the legislative foundation of race-based social inequalities. Given the new agenda, I mixed together my American Ethnicity course – to address the history called for – and my Race and Racism course – to keep the "significance" of it all in organizing our social reality in focus. As I marched my students through the "histories" of America's race and ethnic communities, I made sure to highlight selected pieces of legislation that defined the experiences of different groups, like the internment of Japanese Americans and the immigration prohibitions and residential segregations that made Chinatowns a visible part of our oldest cities. I made sure that they were aware of the massive body of legislation that dispossessed Native Americans of their land. Yet what struck me about the new class was that, unlike the one that preceded it, large sections of 100 students were offered. Over time I came to recognize the importance of where students sat in their engagement with the course content. In lecture halls with three sections of seating and two sets of steps leading in and out to the room, from the bottom of the room in front of the blackboards, I would gaze at the young faces that would remain nameless to me throughout the semester. The students that were most interested in what I had to say sat in the center three rows closest to me. The second group of active participants sat in the front rows to my right; the students on the left were avid note-takers but they were unlikely to talk. Students who were not racially white or Black were scattered throughout the room, sometimes seated in pairs or groups of three. What struck me about them was the often intense gaze with which they hung on every word that came out of my mouth. They seemed to recognize that I was telling them things that they needed to know, but there was often a sense of disbelief, shock, regret and/ or fear that would creep into the expressions on their faces. They were non-participants in our class discussions, but without question, they were paying attention. The rebels, the nay-sayers, the challengers and the disbelievers sat in the center of the room in the third or fourth row from the doors. These were the students that would allow me to get into my lecture, almost all the way through my Powerpoint, or my effort to engage the class in a discussion of a reading or a film, and then one of them would raise their hand and the challenge would begin. I would walk up the steps on whatever side that would allow me to be near to the speaker, listening as I walked, sometimes asking them to repeat their question or comment, sometimes repeating their words to ensure that they were heard by everyone, sometimes stopping when I reached their row to offer my response there, sometimes turning and walking back down the steps as I answered. These rooms were interesting in that, for the most part, they allowed for a type of distancing to be structured into the delivery and receiving of course content. In the rooms of 20 or 30 students, the information of the course hit them; our engagement in the telling and receiving of our national insanity of racism, prejudice and discrimination was palpable. But in this large

Feeling Teaching Race 91

room, the energies of anger, fear, frustration, regret, distress and sorrow about the implications of what was being told could be diffused into the atmosphere without being acknowledged, without bouncing off of our hearts (mine and my students) in a way that would allow us to acknowledge the sorrow, the fear, the regret and the persistent distress that frames our lives as Americans because of our race-based insanity.

4. Pop-up Class and the Race Requirement

In recent years I have been regularly scheduled to teach undergraduates a course that I think of as "race lite." Race is there but in the touchy, feely way of individual identity and personal experience. Theoretically, the course is grounded in social constructionism and identity. The substantive purpose of the course is to reinforce students' understanding of the sociological research process, the logic of research methodology and the structure used in the reporting of research findings. The overwhelming majority of the readings are qualitative research articles about socially relevant identities (e.g., gender, sexuality, immigrant identity, American nationality). The articles vary by race categories. In combination with theoretical readings about social constructionism are methods articles about autoethnography. Some of the research reports are autoethnographies, and others are not. The goal is to have students complete an autoethnography research project that results in a paper that adheres to the structure of a research article. Across the semester, they write research memos, we have discussions about the progress of their projects and they do a formal presentation of their project and findings at the end of the semester. The value of the class is that they become consciously aware of the content and meanings that are embedded in human interactions. They develop a sociological perspective in that they contextualize meaning by social settings and the actors who are engaged in interactions. They gain insight into how their interactions frame and shape their experiences and their interpretations of their experiences. There is a part of me that really appreciates watching them learn and come to terms with the content and meanings of their experiences and that they gain an understanding of the implications of it all for themselves. I think that they walk away from the class with an empowering sociological insight that will benefit them in achieving their goals, thereby improving their quality of life. But, this is race lite, a "pop-up class" that doesn't address the large-scale societal implication of the organization of race identities in the persistence of race-based inequalities. I never mention the social implications and transformations that fall between the *Plessy v. Ferguson* decision and *Brown v. The Board of Education*. The social reality that they created in our past and present has implications for how they experience their identities, but the focus is on their experience of identity and not the larger social structures that frame them. Between theory, methods, data collection, analysis and interpretation, there is no room to have them read Richard Wright's "The Ethics of Living Jim Crow" from *Uncle Tom's Children*

92 *Feeling Teaching Race*

Wright (1938). So they have no sense of the history of hard racial boundaries of segregation that inform their current encounters with seemingly soft, maybe invisible, ones. Nor do they read Langston Hughes' "Father and Son" from *The Ways of White Folks* (1934), so they don't know the sound and insanity of the lynch mob that murders the son of a white man and a Black woman, because he sought to acknowledge his father in public. So those who are now referred to as biracial don't know the "rule of hypodescent" and the penalty of death for its violation. I am certain that they need to know some of this, but there is no time, space or requirement in the pop-up race/race lite of today's washing away of the persistence of white supremacy and the telling of the full story. I know that I have taught them something of what they need to know to get their degree, but I am also certain that I have failed with regard to the racist truths about their identities. The part of me that wants to scream this truth so that they are all prepared for the realities of the United States has been silenced. It is the part of me that cries inside while I speak, as I did in that UVA classroom.

Conclusion

In my heart of hearts having to tell people who are someplace between their late teens and early twenties that all is not fair in the United States and the lack of "fairness" is rationalized by skin color is, for me, the most heartbreaking and insane thing that is required of me as a professor. Yet, I also know that failing to tell them, failing to give them a hint, however subtle, is a disservice to them without regard to their skin color. The student who is white is just as harmed by racism as those who are not white. They are harmed because they have been lied to about the values and ideals of our nation. Their skin color may give them decent to excellent opportunities and a corresponding quality of life. Yet, they have been lied to about our nation, its values and their accomplishments. Something about who they are is a lie. For those who are not white, the threat is insanity, of never quite figuring out "why" they are less than even when they have the material accouterments of how we define success. And, when they don't have them, the suffering of their existence denies the acknowledgment of their humanity. This is what I have to know, what I have to understand, what I have to communicate. My heart breaks, and my tears are real. I am, for what it is worth, the Black girl at the front of the room.

Vaso

Feeling Race as a White Teacher

I imagine the students perceive me as a person with privilege and power because I am white and their professor. In this aura of privilege, I can hide my inadequacies, my brokenness, and present myself as a consummate professor filled with facts and ideas. Yet this confidence and easy feeling is suspended

Feeling Teaching Race 93

when discussions in the classroom are about racial injustice, police brutality, xenophobia and the mass incarceration of Black, Brown and Latino youth. The denial of racism by students, likely immigrant ones, is also wrought with emotion and disconcertion. When I teach my Race and Ethnic Relations course, I am in explosive territory, vigilant and on the lookout for words that might ignite an offense or fight.

Vis a vis my students' dark experiences of living in a racist world, I am compelled to admit to my whiteness despite my inclination not to be identified with it. Treading carefully, as a white teacher professing academic knowledge about race to students of color, I am tasked with leaving space on the classroom floor for the students to express their experiences and concerns about living in a racist America. My whiteness can be an obstacle as, I imagine, the social expectations the students impose on me as a white woman. The white woman is socially distant, I hear in my imagination, the white woman is not one of us. What does she know about living in a racist world?

A Day at the Beginning of the Semester

A day at the beginning of the semester often went like this. The students resisted me and my lesson. I felt the suspicion of the Black and Brown faces in the room, as a white woman teaching about race and the ethnic groups to which they belong. I sought to engage them by directing a question, for example, to a student, who I *assumed* to be a particular racial or ethnic identification, a question about *her/his people*; the student shrugged her shoulders as if to say, "Why are you asking me?" I had expectations that students would be enthusiastic about learning about race and ethnicity in America, about learning all this about themselves. They seemed indifferent or perhaps, the weight of the topic was daunting and frightening. I figured the students were underprepared for college and for the big ideas a college education demands. Their eyes just glazed over at me as I explained the Marxist interpretation of race and ethnicity, that racism and ethnic prejudice is a myth, an ideology rooted in capitalist class locations. I asked for a comment, but no one answered. I worried, felt their judgment and myself withdrawing my enthusiasm for the lesson.

Spotlight on My Whiteness

To put a spotlight on race and show students that even white people are a part of one, I described my white privilege, taking direction from Peggy McIntosh's (2016) "Unpacking the Invisible Knapsack," where she asks white people to interrogate their whiteness. "I hand over my credit card to the cashier," I explained, "without feeling that the cashier might think it's stolen since I am white and supposedly trustworthy," or, I said, "I can approach a police officer with a concern and sense of privilege and believe I won't be perceived with suspicion." I explained how, as a white woman with privilege, I move in the world

94 *Feeling Teaching Race*

with ease because of it. I'm not sure if it worked to help the social distance between the students and me, but it put a spotlight on race and, particularly, the white race in a society that normalizes whiteness. As ethnically Greek, I find the racial binary problematic; however, from the outside, my students saw me as categorically white and my attempts to deny my whiteness by embracing the ethnicity of my identity as primary might be perceived as my wanting to be a marginal member of the society, an "Other" and *appropriating*.

I performed a stereotypical version of white womanhood when I interacted with my students; soft and supportive. I imagined the students perceived me as a nice middle-aged white lady with sensible shoes who cares a lot about her students. Yet, this became a kind of default pattern that is exacerbated when I started feeling diminished when my course on race and ethnicity became overwhelming. The students reacted with both apathy and hostility to the racial and ethnic issues we discussed. I remained motherly yet alert, sometimes permissive and enabling. I didn't show my emotion when they challenged me, even if their attitude was inappropriate. It's a way I got through the course, a way I managed the myriad of feelings in the classroom where students were learning and talking about painful racial and immigration societal issues.

A Semester: On the Days I Taught Race and Ethnicity

My semester was consumed with the preoccupation of how to approach the material and how to motivate the students in my course on Racial and Ethnic Relations. I worked hard on the days leading up to the lessons. On the weekends, I spent hours carefully planning them, clarifying the ideas I wanted to impart, identified my student motivation strategies and the statistical data that supported the lesson. On the days before my class, I was anxious, reviewed my notes and made a list of all that I needed to duplicate for the lesson. In the morning on the days the class met, I was afraid, and I prayed for myself and the lesson. I reminded myself that I knew more than the students did; I knew the history and the theory. Despite the frenzy with which I approached my planning for the lessons, I presented myself to the class as a professional, without emotion and as one with the facts and figures. In the minutes after my classes on race and ethnicity were over, I was relieved, freed from the crippling worry. I would skip to my next class, liberated, eager to teach my Introductory to Sociology section since topics like marriage and family, urbanization and globalization, although potentially explosive, do not provoke the same emotionality I experience when teaching Racial and Ethnic Relations.

At a point in the semester, the students started to trust me. Even if I imagined the students perceived me as racially and ethnically distant, they started *hearing* what I said. It's all too real; they experienced the racism we read and learned about. However, instances of reconciliation surface, such as when a Black student thanked me for "letting us talk," or the thaw I felt when a Nigerian student, who for the first time, in the middle of the semester, seemed eager to speak after staring me down for most of it or when a Palestinian student who seemed to want

Feeling Teaching Race 95

to support me commented that Palestinian Christians "are like Greek [Orthodox] Christians." I will never know what it is like to be Black or Brown in America, but I can guide students to understand their racial location and the way class, gender, ethnicity and sexuality come to shape their life chances and everyday lives.

Conclusion

We have described what we experience in the classroom, the perspectives and emotions that inform and define our efforts to teach college students about the significance of race identities, racialized experiences and racism. We weaved together experiences of objectivity and subjectivity. Objectively, the academic literature, research findings and theories inform the course content. This is information, the knowledge that we want our students to learn. On the other hand, we and our students have brought our race identities with us into the classroom. Everyone in the room has some commonsense knowledge, a subjective understanding, of the social implications of race identities. However, our responsibility to move students past common sense and to the facts and social impact of racism is a daunting one.

In telling our stories, the authors provide evidence that the social salience of race is persistent. As academics, PhDs and sociologists, we bring our credentials in the study of race and racism to bear on our experiences. There is no denying the depth of social change in relation to race identities and systemic race-based social inequalities. We signal this reality as we expose the ways that race still matters in terms of experiences and social inequalities. Moreover, teaching is not a site of pure objectivity. Where subjectivity runs parallel to course content, emotions can inform teaching. As in other interactions, race identity can be a salient factor in the experience of teaching.

References

Black, Marc. 2007. "Fanon and DuBoisian Double Consciousness in Reflections on Fanon: The Violences of Colonialism and Racism, Inner and Global – Conversations with Frantz Fanon on the Meaning of Human Emancipation." *Human Architecture: Journal of the Sociology of Self-Knowledge* V (Special Issue): 393–404.
DuBois, W. E. B. 2008. *The Souls of Black Folk.* Edited by Brent Hayes Edwards. Oxford World's Classics. London, UK: Oxford University Press.
Dunbar, Paul Lawrence. 1895. "We Wear the Mask." In *The Complete Poems of Paul Lawrence Dunbar.* New York, NY: Dodd, Mead, and Company.
Fannon, Frantz. 1952. *Black Skin White Masks.* New York, NY: Grove Press.
Freire, Paulo. 2000. *Pedagogy of the Oppressed.* New York, NY: Continuum.
Hughes, Langston. 1934. *The Ways of White Folks.* New York: A. A. Knopf.
McIntosh, Peggy. 2016. "Unpacking the Invisible Knapsack." In *White Privilege: Essential Readings on the Other Side of Racism,* edited by Paula Rothenberg. New York, NY: Worth Publishers.
Wright, Richard. 1938. *Uncle Tom's Children.* New York: Penguin Books.

Conclusion

Our research provides a multi-vocal presentation of what it means to teach Race Studies courses in a racially neoliberal environment among instructors with different race identities. Through our research, we came to understand the power of the early life story to shape our racial consciousness and the serious implications race had for our lives and communities. Our autoethnographic analysis demonstrates that the consciousness of race identity formation is founded in childhood by adult silence in the presence of racial "others," or the classroom where no one else shares the color of your skin or some other behavioral pattern that lets you know the relevance of skin color. We all felt race even when we were too young to fully understand what it was all about. Our early memories of race and the feelings we experienced as a part of those racial encounters are reflected in the way we came to identify ourselves as racial beings. We all, white, Black, bi-racial, *ethnic* or not, experienced racial tension in our families and came to understand that race was critical in shaping how our families lived and experienced their lives.

From our research, we identified the way race was confusing for us as young children, and how Blackness and whiteness evoked different emotional reactions – anger, fear, power, excitement, beauty. We identified feelings of loneliness, shame, powerlessness, fear and discomfort; for some of us, losing our childhood innocence and self-esteem. We felt whiteness as privilege, dominance, anger, oppression and violence which created life-long suffering and trauma. At the same time, some of us received positive affirmations about being Black and Brown and felt joy, self-love and excitement about being girls of color growing up during the 1960s and 1970s.

When sharing our early race memories, it also quickly became clear that our relationships with race did not always fall easily along racial identity lines. While our racialized identities are formative in shaping the nature of those struggles, there are complexities within each that make our particular battlefields unique. That is to say, the differences in the ways that Adriana, Donna-Marie and Michelle's racialized identities were constructed are many. The same was true for Mary and Vaso. However, the fear of whiteness and white violence was central to the construction of Adriana, Donna-Marie and Michelle's identities.

DOI: 10.4324/9781003442448-5

Conclusion 97

That fear is what kept Adriana's heart palpitating and her voice shaking. That fear, felt by her mother, was what kept Michelle from getting on that bus. That fear is what kept Donna-Marie longing for the safety of her city block. For each of them, their fears were realized but at different times in their lives: at a very young age for Donna-Marie, who experienced terrifying white violence at her home and white prejudice at school; as a coming-of-age teen moving to the highly segregated and unequal city of Wilmington for Adriana; and as a graduate student at UVA for Michelle. This is not to say that white racial dominance wasn't ever present for everyone, but that it "came alive" at different times for the women of color in the group and that it shaped their racial identity formation, which in turn shaped the character of their current racialized identities and what they carry into the Race Studies classroom.

Vaso and Mary also had very different experiences of racial identity construction, a difference informed by the highly salient intersection of ethnic and racial constructions for Vaso that was largely absent for Mary. For Vaso, the fear of whiteness was as salient as the fear of blackness in her early years. It isn't until she begins her relationship with her Black boyfriend, now husband, or when she reacts to the OJ Simpson verdict that she comes to see herself as white. This white identity that she longed for as a youth is now something that she embodies quite reluctantly. This reluctance to see oneself as white, as a part of the problem, comes earlier for Mary. While anti-blackness characterized her earliest experiences with race as her grandma pulled her across the street, her feelings of ambivalence about her own whiteness were implanted by a progressive fourth grade teacher. Yet both Vaso and Mary tried to push the problem of whiteness away, with Vaso holding onto an ethnic Greek and hence not quite white, identity and Mary searching for the "good" white people at every turn. These "reluctant" white identities are what they bring into the Race Studies classroom.

The experience of teaching Race Studies courses must be understood not only with such race identity formations in mind but also within the context of today's racial neoliberalism, where student assumptions of or desires for a post-racial society collide with faculty teachings about systemic racism. We enter our classrooms in a very different era from the one that shaped our own early race experiences. This new era is one where race and racism are not always acknowledged, one where even the most prominent racial theorists argued that the significance of race had declined. This is the era of racial neoliberalism, of "racism without racists," and of colorblindness. This was the new context in which we had to wrestle with our identities and our relationships to race as well as the identities and relationships of those students sitting before us.

The multi-level tensions between what faculty are tasked with teaching and what students are often loath to learn are shaped by these racial identity formations of both faculty and students. The way we as faculty experience these tensions is informed by our early, and unique, relationships to race, in a time before racial neoliberalism was ideologically and structurally embedded in our

98 *Conclusion*

society. The same is true for our students in that they come in with their own experiences, identities and relationships to race, the majority of whom were raised during a time when racial neoliberalist ideas were deeply systemic. Our courses disrupt neoliberal "common sense" assumptions about race identities, racial groups and race-based social inequalities. In other words, teaching and learning are the sites of disruption. We are literally telling our students, all of them, without regard to their race, what they don't want to know. We are telling them that race identities do matter. We are telling them that race continues to be a variable that explains social inequalities given variations in race identities. In other words, we tell them that their race identity does matter. We tell them that systemic race-based inequalities are not only persistent but there is something that is persistent in our ways of being as a society and a nation that makes this so. They may hear us, they may not hear us, they may decide that what we are saying does not apply to them. However, we know the truth in the data, in the statistics, in the research findings and in their implications. We know that what we are telling them is true.

Struggling with student resistance to faculty instruction is, of course, nothing new. Students "resist" in a variety of ways by not turning in their work or by not participating in class, falling asleep or texting on their phones. Managing this type of resistance can be both stressful and time-consuming, particularly when we are teaching a large number of students. Yet these are stressors that "come with the job." We expect that not all students will do exactly as we ask them to do, and we expect to have to manage those students. But the student resistance we experience in Race Studies courses, while expected by us as instructors with many years of teaching under our belts, is an expectation that goes largely unacknowledged or perhaps unknown by our larger institutions and society due to the power of racial neoliberalism. Our experiences in the Race Studies classroom are inextricably linked to our experiences in our racialized society, a society that values whiteness above all else yet professes to value us all equally. The battles we experience in the Race Studies classroom are reflective of the battles we experience outside of the classroom. The fear, anger, sadness and determination are with us in and out of the classroom. We struggle to manage that fear and that anger both in and out of the classroom. Yet no matter how hard we each may try to disassociate from our racial feelings and our non-professor racial selves in the classroom, each of us discovered that our racialized experiences and identities are a constant presence when we teach Race Studies. At times we try to create emotional, and maybe even physical, walls between the classroom, ourselves, and our students to try to ward off fatigue, fear, exasperation, longing and despair. Yet, even after all of these years, the struggle remains very "real." We hear this in Adriana's voice, Donna-Marie's fear, Mary's anxiety, Michelle's sorrow and Vaso's disappointment.

Teaching Race Studies courses in this socio-historical context feels like a constant battle to all of us, each and every day. These battles are complicated,

Conclusion 99

both spoken and unspoken. There are the battles we have with ourselves as we stand on that classroom stage: Should I try to don the proverbial "mask," "stick to the facts" ("shut up and dribble!") and be "matter of fact"? Am I even capable of doing so? Or should I allow myself to be vulnerable, share my truth and acknowledge my pain? And then there are the battles with our students: Should I challenge them? Ignore them? Put them in their place? Validate them? There are no easy answers to these questions, and yet more importantly, in this era of racial neoliberalism, these questions are rarely being asked because our racialized subjective identities are not acknowledged institutionally or otherwise. Clearly though, these tensions amount to a more emotionally and pedagogically complex experience than is found when teaching a course where our own identities aren't so intertwined with the subject matter at hand. It's hard to imagine that anyone ever believed or imagined that these courses wouldn't present a unique struggle for instructors. Our classrooms are social experiments filled with manifold explosives that detonate in new and unexpected ways every year with every new racial struggle, "incident" or hashtag. Our collective pedagogical brilliance cannot stop the bleeding.

Thus one of the primary takeaways from our research is that classrooms are not objective spaces but ones where subjective actors are engaging in a racialized context with racialized beings. As scholars and social scientists, we are asked to approach phenomena with an objective and emotional distance; however, in this book, we challenge this approach and consider the significance of emotionality and the embedded racial identities which we bring to the classroom. There is nothing emotionless about teaching Race Studies coursesI-facade of objectivity we come to adopt as educators belies this emotionality and hinders an understanding of racial neoliberalism that shapes these classroom experiences. In our common goal of dissecting systems of oppression, we have all felt soul-crushing despair, apprehension, exhaustion, rage and physical pain, despite our different racial and ethnic identities. At the same time, we also experience the joy and exhilaration of teaching. Teaching about systemic racism, race-based discrimination, resistance and revolution makes us feel bold and proud.

In hindsight, these findings seem obvious; of course, these classes are uniquely complicated and fraught with faculty emotion, and of course, the formation of faculty racial identities is central to this experience! However, given that these courses operate within a system of higher education that is beholden to neoliberal understandings, we are encouraged to believe that neither student identities nor our own identities matter. What this project tells us is that faculty identity matters, not just in terms of student or institutional evaluations, workload or "burn-out" but also in terms of what faculty bring to the classroom and hence how they will feel and experience the classroom. Our own experiences with racial segregation, with anti-Blackness, with fear of white people, with Black pride and with racial identity confusion are present with us in the

100 *Conclusion*

classroom as we teach about these same issues. In doing this autoethnography, we were able to not only reflect upon what we feel when teaching but also to understand how those feelings connected to how we came to know ourselves as "raced," as Black, white and biracial.

When teaching courses in which subjective faculty identities are also the object of study, it is incumbent upon both instructor and institution to examine those identities; to know what faculty are "bringing." This examination, we suggest, will benefit not only pedagogical "effectiveness" but the well-being of instructors and the overall institutional goals that shape these course offerings. Further, this book suggests that the autoethnographic method offers a useful way to begin that examination. Faculty teaching Race Studies courses should consider doing their own racial autoethnographies so they can explore their own racial identity formations. Uncovering and reflecting upon our early relationships to race – and the impact of race on decisions and experiences in the classroom – allowed us to reclaim our identities from our workplace, meaning that although our institutions don't want to talk about our identities mattering, we know our racial identities do matter.

It wasn't until this project that we were able to analyze the presence of these identities inside our classrooms, a presence that institutions of higher education would rather not explore. And it wasn't until this project that we were able to explore how our identities were formed, an exploration we ourselves were at first hesitant to do. Doing this made us realize that not only can the experience of teaching Race Studies be traumatizing, but that, in fact, it can often be re-traumatizing. On the flip side, this experience can also be redeeming and empowering in ways that make the pain of our early relationships to race less burdensome. Regardless, faculty teaching Race Studies classes should be prepared not only for inevitable student resistance but for the myriad of ways in which our identities will inevitably become a part of the pedagogy.

Miller et al. (2019) suggest the importance of making emotional labor visible to higher education administrators and to those who are planning for this career. And further, "Academic leaders, departments, and faculty members should discuss how emotional work is recognized and considered within hiring, promotion, and tenure decisions" (500). Our work offers a rich and varied illustration of that emotional work and a clear foundation for that essential discussion. That foundation is that faculty racial identities matter, and they matter most significantly when teaching Race Studies courses. But to understand how they matter, we must draw our attention to identity formation. Practically, this book asks institutions to consider the interactions between faculty racial identity, socio-political realities and the experiences associated with Race Studies courses for both instructors and students. In other words, this book reminds us all that finding effective pedagogical tools and strategies for Race Studies classes must center the racial identity formations of its instructors. Finally, this book demands a spotlight be put upon how educational institutions can support faculty teaching these courses, courses that we believe are essential in the larger effort to build a racially just society.

Reference

Miller, Ryan S., Cathy D. Howell, and Laura E. Struve. 2019. " 'Constantly, Excessively, and All the Time': The Emotional Labor of Teaching Diversity Courses." *The International Journal of Teaching and Learning in Higher Education* 31 (3) : 491–502. http://files.eric.ed.gov/fulltext/EJ1245085.pdf.

Epilogue

We began writing this book before the COVID-19 pandemic shut us down in March 2020 and abruptly disrupted the flow of our work and face-to-face classes. Pivoting quickly, we faced the challenge of meeting and writing virtually and adapted our pedagogies to remote learning in a time of fear, uncertainty and social isolation. We learned new technology to communicate with each other and tried to capture student interest using innovative strategies. We taught in virtual classrooms yet often did not see student faces, as many sat behind video screens with cameras off and microphones muted. Together, yet isolated in new and confounding ways, we all watched the harsh realities of systemic racism unfold as we consumed the news on a 24-hour media loop. Racism wasn't a new phenomenon, but now it was panoptic. Locked inside, racism was omnipresent in real-time: captured by iPhone cameras and Facebook Live, posted on social media, shared thousands of times and replayed in a never-ending cycle. There was no escape.

"I can't breathe," George Floyd lay on the ground handcuffed, pleading for his life, as a policeman pressed his knee on his neck and purposely killed him. The smiling face of Breonna Taylor, gunned down in a barrage of 32 shots fired into her apartment by seven plainclothes police officers after they forcibly entered with a battering ram, flashed across our laptops. The constant barrage and ubiquitous videos of police atrocities and attempted cover-ups reached a tipping point across the world, provoking moral outrage and an international clarion call for social justice as demands for police reform moved from the streets to state legislatures to Congress.

Horrified by the images promenading across our screens, protests began in Minneapolis on May 26, 2020, and in the following months, between 15 million and 26 million people across the country took to the streets, averaging close to 140 protests a day, in challenges to the State-sanctioned murder of Black and Brown people, and the neoliberal myth of a colorblind society (Buchanan, Quoctrung, and Patel 2020). "Black Lives Matter!" organized in 2013, now resounded across the world, and the largest mass protest movement in US history toppled, removed and renamed close to 170 Confederate

DOI: 10.4324/9781003442448-6

Epilogue 103

symbols; renewed calls for legislative action on reparations; and gave birth to coalitions that disrupted the fabric of US society by organizing, strategizing, developing and promoting policies and laws for more racial justice (Burch et al. 2021). For instance, New York opened up police disciplinary records to the angry public, new laws banning chokeholds and "No Knock" warrants were instated and calls to "defund the police" rang out across the country, with the Minneapolis City Council pledging to fully dismantle their police force.

We were a part of this world on fire. Everyday people, led often by our youth, demanded America deliberate on what it meant to be Black in the US. This movement was marked by many whites and other people of color participating in the protests. More than 40% of US counties witnessed protests, and in 95% of the counties where protests were held, the county was majority white, and in close to three-quarters of the counties, more than 75% of people were white (Buchanan, Quoctrung, and Patel 2020). Similar to the Civil War, the Civil Rights Movement and the Black, Latino, Asian and Indigenous Movements of years past, America was once again forced into racial reckoning. BIPOC activists and their allies beheld their humanity and demanded recognition. In this reckoning, we felt agentic and powerful.

We cheered historical racial achievements and were optimistic about achieving political change, but the backlash or counter-reckoning was, and remains, "fierce" (Glaude 2022). Joe Biden defeated Donald Trump in the 2020 presidential election, which garnered more votes than any other election in US history, but President Trump refused to acknowledge his defeat, calling on his followers to "Stop the Steal" and encouraging insurrection. The world watched as a violent mob stormed the United States Capitol on January 6, 2021, challenging the 2020 presidential election results. Fearless and undaunted, Trump's support of the insurrectionists was viewed in real-time. He encouraged his supporters to head to the Capitol Building, armed with baseball bats, shields and chemical spray. He cheered them on as they used their weapons to knock down barriers, break through doors, attack the police and eventually enter the Capitol's hallowed halls, determined to overthrow democracy. He laughed as they invaded the private offices of elected representatives, telling them he would join them shortly. Brazenly, insurgents rushed through the doors of the empty Senate Chambers. One man stretched out, gesticulated and smiled, resting his dirty boots on top of the desk of the Speaker of the House, posing for the cameras. In this sacred political space, American terrorists stood at the podium in a show of victory. Looters carried the Confederate flag, swastikas and other symbols of white supremacy. As we began another semester of teaching Race Studies courses in the shadow of this insurrection, we knew that some of our students would see these Americans as patriots. Over the next two years, we watched as more and more policies presented in the aftermath of George Floyd's murder, such as defunding the police, were ridiculed and defanged by both Democrats and Republicans. We knew that many of our students would feel similar sentiments.

104 *Epilogue*

As a country, we have had innumerable opportunities to confront and tackle racism at a national level, yet once again, as Glaude (2022) writes, "At every moment in which a new America is on the verge of being reborn, the umbilical cord of white supremacy has been wrapped around the baby's neck, choking the life out of it." Glaude's commentary also speaks directly to what is happening in our educational institutions.

In addition to the California State University system's decision to require ethnic studies, in the aftermath of the police murder of George Floyd, statewide Black Student Union coalitions were formed, Black Lives Matter curriculums were in demand and in 2021, Delaware passed HB 198, which mandated each school district and charter school teach Black American History from kindergarten through grade 12. This latest progress in educational reform had been building since 2013 when the Black Lives Matter movement emerged following the not-guilty verdict for George Zimmerman in the murder of Trayvon Martin. The BLM in-school curriculum was implemented first in 2016 and grew from there. In 2019, one year before Minneapolis police killed George Floyd, the 1619 project made its debut in the *New York Times* and found its way into classrooms around the country. But it wasn't until after George Floyd was murdered by police, and we witnessed the biggest national uprising in our lifetimes, that we saw then-President Trump push back with not one, but two executive orders attacking educational reform. One order called for a "1776 commission" to "restore patriotic" education in our schools – a direct attack on the 1619 project – and the other sought to ban DEI training and any education that suggested that the United States was inherently racist – a direct attack on Critical Race Theory (CRT). Soon after, in early 2021, Idaho Governor Brad Little became the first Governor to sign a bill into law that prevented educators from teaching tenets "often found in critical race theory." By the summer of 2021, twelve more states (Arizona, Arkansas, Georgia, Indiana, Iowa, Oklahoma, Rhode Island, Mississippi, South Dakota, Tennessee, Texas and Utah) introduced similar legislation. Then, Florida's Stop Woke Act took effect in July 2022, limiting DEI-related training in schools and in the workplace. This legislation paved the way for the rejection of Advanced Placement African American studies courses, bans on books in school libraries and continued efforts to remove funding for DEI programs in Florida and beyond.

As Republican candidates begin to announce their bids for the 2024 presidential election, heated debates on educational curricula continue, yet Republicans seem to have a consensus in their opposition to education reform for racial justice. Former President Trump has promised to eliminate federal funding for schools that teach critical race theory, and Florida Gov. Ron DeSantis is promising to "make Florida America" by banning all "woke" ideology and teaching throughout the country. His vitriolic remarks caused the National Association for the Advancement of Colored People in May 2023 to issue a travel advisory to Florida, following in the footsteps of Equality Florida and the Florida Immigration Coalition.

The steadfast refusal to acknowledge, teach about and reparate historical racism in the US and the insidious ways in which contemporary racism holds Black and Brown people hostage is that umbilical cord of which Glaude (2022) speaks. Rachelle P. Walensky, Director of the Centers for Disease Control and Prevention, recently declared racism a public health threat, arguing that the real "unaddressed epidemic impacting public health is racism" (2021, pg. 1). Inoculated against one crippling pandemic, the national refusal to confront the deadliest pandemic of all, white supremacy, has resulted in students returning to face-to-face, partisan, volatile and undeniably stressed-out classrooms. The numerous political attacks on teaching about the realities of systemic racism are indeed choking all of us who are teaching Race Studies courses. Yet, we continue the struggle, the struggle to teach the truth, to tell our students that race matters, that racism is systemic and that it is up to all of us to end this pandemic once and for all.

References

Buchanan, L., B. Quoctrung, and J. Patel. 2020. "Black Lives Matter May Be the Largest Movement in US History." *The New York Times*, July 3.

Burch, Audra, Amy Harmon, Sabrina Tavernise, and Emily Badger. 2021. "The Death of George Floyd Reignited a Movement: What Happens Now?" *The New York Times*, April 20.

Glaude, Eddie. 2022. "Black Progress, White Anger, John F. Kennedy Jr. Forum, March 30, 2022, in Liz Mineo." *The Harvard Gazette*, April 1.

Walensky, Rachelle P. 2021. "Media Statement from CDC Director on Racism and Health." *Center for Disease Control*, April 8. https://www.cdc.gov/media/releases/2021/s0408-racism-health.html.

Appendix: Methodological Reflections

Doing collaborative autoethnography (CAE) is methodologically and logistically challenging. Fortunately, Chang, Ngunjiri, and Hernandez (2016) "wrote the book" on this research method, which served as a constant guiding force in not only helping us figure out what to do, but also in its assurance to us that the obstacles we were encountering should be both expected and surmountable. We met as a group for the first time on March 11, 2017, to decide if we were all really ready to embark on this project together – we were ready. Our primary research goal was to find out how our early relationships with race interacted with our teaching race experience. Thus we decided we would begin by gathering data about our early relationship with race.

The central data point in the autoethnographic method is deceptively simple: study yourself as "self-memory and recollection" are the primary sources of data collection (Chang, Ngunjiri, and Hernandez 2016, 74). Each of us turned inward for our individual self-reflection and writing (preliminary data collection). We began by writing what we could remember, and when we couldn't remember or maybe didn't want to remember, we asked those we thought might know and we consulted "archival materials" (Chang, Ngunjiri, and Hernandez 2016). We consulted old photographs, old friends and family, old stories and writings, old letters and old places to help us remember how race felt before it became so central to our professional careers. For example, we asked siblings to confirm/disconfirm our childhood memories. We visited our childhood schools and neighborhoods and contacted old teachers. We revisited old journal and diary writings. We remembered ourselves in a middle school uniform staring at Rolling Stones posters taped on our bedroom wall. We remembered ourselves in tank tops and hot pants, exuding the confidence of Black beauty. We remembered being victims of racist ridicule and violence by other kids and adults alike. We remembered racist grandpas who loved us very much. We researched the TV shows that were so important to us, but that had been largely forgotten until we began reflecting on the development of our understanding of race. We often utilized what Chang (2008) identified as "inventorying" exercises, where we made lists of childhood race memories and lists of people who

Appendix: Methodological Reflections 107

were a part of those memories and could then pull from those lists to dig deeper into the memories that offered the most insight into our experiences with race. We were engaging in subsequent data collection on our early relationships with race after group consultation and preliminary data collection on our experiences teaching race, where we delved into old email communications, syllabi, readings and lectures. We all engaged in this process of reflection and consultation until we decided we had a good enough understanding of our experiences of race prior to and while teaching Race Studies courses to write something.

As others have noted, the CAE process is anything but a linear process but more of what Chang, Ngunjiri, and Hernandez (2016) call a "borderless process of data collection, analysis, interpretation, and writing" (113). This was true for us as well though we did make a very intentional plan to "begin writing our data drafts" after our initial periods of reflection and consultation. Nonetheless, when one has 24/7 access to their research "subject" it is hard to actually stop collecting data or even to stop re-analyzing and re-interpreting said data! Yet we did indeed begin writing and then shared our writing drafts of our "feeling race" data chapter with each other through Google drive and planned to meet in person to discuss these writings. This "concurrent" model of each of us working on our "Feeling Race" chapter at the same time, then moving to our "Teaching Race" chapter and then to our final "Feeling Teaching Race" chapter worked pretty well. Between drafts, we were offering feedback to each other using Google docs and face-to-face meetings every other month. By January 2018, some ten months after our first meeting, we had each drafted our three data chapters and read and offered comments on everyone else's data chapter drafts. Data chapter revisions were at varying stages and would remain that way for the duration of our process.

It's not clear that any of us were quite prepared for emotions that came up either with our own writing or with reading each other's writings. Thus, when it came time to "ask probing questions," we often did so not as confident research investigators but as empathetic friends. Indeed, it often sounded as if we were each other's counselors vs. methodological collaborators – i.e., *Well, were you angry or sad? Did your parents know how this felt? That must have been so confusing!* Once we got more comfortable and familiar with everyone's stories and reminded ourselves that these meetings were an important component of the CAE method, we were able to turn to more academic probing or what Chang, Ngunjiri, and Hernandez (2016) call "collaborative meaning making." For some of us, however, it remained difficult to offer critical feedback, as we might easily do with a student, on our friends' emotional narratives. It felt out of place, condescending or perhaps too invasive. Critical feedback signals that the author has done something wrong or they need to improve on something. How do you offer this type of critique when the author is your friend and has narrated their experiences that reveal witnessing, participating in or being the target of racialized injustice and dehumanization?

108   *Appendix: Methodological Reflections*

Another complication we faced was figuring out the timing and balance between individual writing and revising and group reading and discussion. As Chang, Ngunjiri, and Hernandez (2016) note, too much of the former, without the latter, can create too much variation in each individual "data set." We found this to be true particularly when working on our second data chapter, "Teaching Race," where some of us were focused almost fully on course content and others on classroom dynamics. When we began tackling the third data chapter, "Feeling Teaching Race," we probably could have saved ourselves considerable revision time with more discussion at the outset, as so many buried experiences were unearthed through reading and offering feedback to each other. This was perhaps the most painful chapter to write and to read, yet also the most bonding for us as a group. Gathering data for this chapter at the same time that we were teaching these courses was a strange and moving experience. We were "in our feelings" while trying to identify those feelings. For the most part, it seems we had all been operating under the assumption that it was best not to be so present with those feelings when trying to teach Race Studies courses, that this emotional reckoning would make our jobs only that much harder. Thus when we did force ourselves to sit and reflect upon what we generally feel in those rooms, fear, anxiety and anger, it was, indeed, often quite painful. Our grown-up vulnerabilities and insecurities were named and we're now up for collective viewing – yikes.

With our three data chapters drafted, our creative selves returned to our academic training – to analyze our data and work on clarifying and refining our research questions and our problem statement and engage in what could only be described as a highly inefficient "strategic" review of the literature. This is where collaboration became chaos. The goal was to "unpack meanings" from themes we discovered across our data (Chang, Ngunjiri, and Hernandez 2016, 98). But we also understood, as others have suggested, that our individual "stories" are often inherently analytic/interpretive, such that we may indeed have been engaging in meaning making prior to this step. Particularly because of our continued desire to stay close to the analytic autoethnographic camp, there always seemed to be some degree of concerted interpretation among us. At times, some of us questioned why we needed so much emphasis on the analytic framing of our wonderfully rich data, while others insisted our work would be insufficient without such an emphasis. Thus, while our data chapters reveal a significant amount of Imaginative-Creative (IC), aka evocative, writing, our overall work most closely aligns with the Analytic-Interpretive (AI) writing style in that we stick to a pretty standard format of offering our research purpose, research questions, literature review, method, findings and conclusions (Chang, Ngunjiri, and Hernandez 2016, 128).

Returning to academic writing also meant our first attempt at truly collaborative writing. Lowry, Curtis and Lowry (2004) define collaborative writing as "an iterative and social process that involves a team focused on a common objective that negotiates, coordinates and communicates during the creation

Appendix: Methodological Reflections 109

of a common document" (72). Though we had been collaborating, we were writing our own data chapters about our own lives, and now we were planning on writing the same chapters together, and this proved to be much more complicated with another pretty steep learning curve as we had little experience in collaborative research. In the end, some non-data sections were written as "group single author" writing, where one person writes on behalf of the group, and other parts were written as "partitioned" writing, where we split up subsections between us (Chang, Ngunjiri, and Hernandez 2016, 123). Decisions about who should write what sometimes followed a "horizontal" division of sections, meaning with no consideration of the particular author's skill sets/knowledge, and at other times, we used a "stratified" division, such as when it was clear that one of us had the greatest experience writing about race theory (Stratton 1989 cited in Chang, Ngunjiri, and Hernandez 2016, 123). During this time, there were, of course, varied data interpretations emerging – i.e., the role of neoliberalism in the classroom/university; the role of "presumed objectivity" of both faculty and students in the classroom/university; or the overall presence of an affective realm of the classroom. As these variations continued to emerge, we got frustrated. We needed to find a lane and stick to it, but we weaved from lane to lane for miles, which is why reviewing the literature was so taxing and inefficient. It's hard enough in doing solo research to decide how to theoretically situate your work, but when there were five of us with different theoretical familiarities and interpretations, things got really messy. Of course, this is also where some very important work happened despite the many literature rabbit holes we went down. As Chang, Ngunjiri, and Hernandez (2016) assure, "Undertaking a search of the literature during your interpretation phase enables you to find explanatory frameworks and to engage the marketplace of published ideas by extending, critiquing, illustrating, and challenging existing explanations" (113). Let's just say our marketplace was more like the Mall of America. We went up and down many theoretical and conceptual paths before settling on the framework of racial neoliberalism. It is this concept, this context, that seemed to offer the most explanatory power in understanding all of our feelings and experiences when teaching race studies courses. Thus, while collaboration certainly made the process of settling into a theoretical framework somewhat chaotic, it also allowed us to feel confident in where we landed as a collective.

By digging deep into our own childhood relationships with race, our pedagogical choices and our feelings about our classroom experiences, we engaged in this collaborative autoethnographic process to analyze the emotional experience of teaching Race Studies classes. This process involved revealing to ourselves and to each other experiences and emotions associated with teaching mostly young adults about the racialized nature of American society. Many of these experiences and emotions had previously gone unexamined, denied or ignored for fear that acknowledgment would be undesirable or perhaps unbearable. We shared with each other our pasts, both in writing and in conversation

110 *Appendix: Methodological Reflections*

and how we felt about those pasts – we stirred up each other's memories, unsettled each other's assumptions and pushed each other to go to the most vulnerable of places – not just to understand ourselves but to understand the overall emotional experience of teaching Race Studies courses, courses where we must experience race both objectively as subject matter and subjectively as faculty with different racialized subjectivities and consciousnesses.

References

Chang, Heewon. 2008. *Autoethnography as Method.* Walnut Creek, CA: Left Coast Press.
Chang, Heewon, Faith Ngunjiri, and Kathy-Ann C. Hernandez. 2016. *Collaborative Autoethnography.* London: Routledge.
Lowry, Paul Benjamin, Aaron Curtis, and Michelle Lowry. 2004. "Building a Taxonomy and Nomenclature of Collaborative Writing to Improve Interdisciplinary Research and Practice." *Journal of Business Communication* 41 (1): 66–99. https://doi.org/10.1177/0021943603259363.
Stratton, Charles R. 1989. "Collaborative Writing in the Workplace." *IEEE Transactions on Professional Communication* 32 (3): 178–82. https://doi.org/10.1109/47.31626.

Index

Note: Page locators in *italics* indicate a figure.

activists 1, 15, 54, 60, 63, 75, 103
advantages/disadvantages 3, 74
affirmative action 3, 56, 65, 86
African: American 21, 34, 63–65, 67–69;
    ancestry 2, 63–66, 69, 87–89;
    history *25*, 51, 67, 69
Aiello, Danny 34
Alexander, Michelle 53
American culture 4, 22, 40
American Dream 47
American Ethnicity 76, 88–90
American Negro 63
analytic reflexivity 8–9
Anderson, Leon 8
Angelou, Maya 41
anti-racist/anti-racism 4, 15, 21, 31, 67
armor 75, 79–80
Asian: descent 2, 65, 88–89, 103;
    stereotyping 58
authority 5, 16, 22, 80
autoethnography 7–8, 91, 100; *see also*
    collaborative autoethnography
avoidance 32

Baca, Judith 52
Bailey, John 19
barriers 3, 103
behavior: color-conscious 31; distracting
    64; group 46, 76; intimidating
    5, 82, 86
BIPOC activists 103
Black, Marc 79
Black: Americans 35, 65–66, 76; beauty
    36, 106; Community 64, 87;
    history 16, *25*; power 14, 36, 39,
    52–53

Black Lives Matter 62, 102, 104–105
blackness 1, 31, 38, 43, 64, 87–89, 97
Black Power Movement 14, 52–53
blues (music genre) 15
Bohm, Adriana Leela 12, *14*, 43, 45, 75,
    96–98
Bon Jovi 34
boundaries: racial 39, 43, 88, 92; social
    3, 13
boycotts 14, 52
Brown, John 54
Brownness 14, 16, 20, 24
brown skin 15, 37–38, 42
Burton, Levar 33
Byng, Michelle 35, 43, 63, 87, 96–98

CAE *see* collaborative ethnography
California State University 1
capitalism 16
cartoon characters 36–37
Cazenave, Noel 4
CCCC *see* Cecil County Community
    College
Cecil County Community College 22
Centers for Disease Control 105
Chacon, Soledad 51
Che`-Lumumba School *14*, 15–16, 21, 54
Chicago Cubs 32
Chicano 52
Chin Foo, Wong 62
Civil Rights: era 31, 35, 36, *36*;
    legislation 3, 35, 65
Civil Rights Act 1957/1968 65
Civil Rights Movement 2, 13, 35, 37, 54,
    89, 103
Clarke, Breena 53

112 *Index*

class/classes: activities in 50, 57; race 35, 45–46, 49, 57, 60; social class 3, 13, 88; working-class 16, 19, 26, 31, 88
classism 15
Cleaver, Eldridge 41
Cleaver, Kathleen 52
CMR *see* complete member – researcher status
Coates, Ta-Nehisi 53
collaborative ethnography 8–9
Collins, Patricia Hill 67
colorblind 60–61, 69–70, 97, 102
color blind racism 69
colorism 69
coming of age 24, 97
complete member – researcher status 8
confidence 16, 24, 60, 75, 81, 92
confident 14, 77, 107, 109
consciousness: color 31, 35–36, 60; racial 4, 13, 16, 96
Correa, Chick 40
Corwin, Thomas 61–62
Critical Race Theory 2, 5, 104
Crockett, Davy 25–26
CRT *see* Critical Race Theory
Cruz, Sophia 52
CSU *see* California State University

Dandridge, Dorothy 37
Davis, Angela 14, 35, 38, 53
Davis, Miles 15
Davis, Troy 61
DCCC *see* Delaware County Community college
de-escalate 78, 80
Delaware County Community College 45, 76
Delta Sigma Theta Sorority, Inc 21
Denny, Reginald 35
Denzin, Norman 7
DeSantis, Ron 104
desegregation 19
DiAngelo, Robin 53
dignity 51, 81
disbelief 28, 32–33, 90
discrimination: history 65, 88–89; institutional 1, 35
Disney World 33
diversity 4, 8, 57, 82–83, 88
Do the Right Thing 34
Dominican 41, 68–69

DuBois, William Edward Burghardt (W.E.B.) 46, 64, 66, 79
Dunbar, Paul Lawrence 79

Elliot, Jane 31
Ellis, Carolyn 7
emotions: defined 4, 95; evoke 8, 34, 75, 78; hidden 80–81; process 48–49, 55
empower/empowerment 36, 39, 51, 57–58, 69, 84, 91, 100
equality 2, 27, 54, 62, 66, 70, 104
ethnic relations 2, 64, 89
ethnic studies 1, 104
ethnicity 41, 43, 68–69, 89, 93–95
exclusion 2, 89
experiences of teaching 2, 87

faculty: identity 5, 99; women of color 5–6
fairness 3, 92
family racism 41
Fanon, Frantz 79
Farrell, Sheila 19
fear: emotional 48, 58, 75, 90–91; fire 26–27, 81; race-based 14, 19, 21, 31–32, 35, 96–97
feeling race 13, 24, 107
feminism 7, 39
fight back 15, 79–80
Fleming, Crystal Marie 53
Foner, Nancy 68
fragility 47, 76
Franklin, Aretha 15
freedom 15, 25, 34, 47, 56
Freire, Paulo 53

garment industry 68
Gaye, Marvin 66
gender 41, 49, 59, 68, 95
Germany 16–17, 38
Ghana 51, 68
Glaude, Eddie 53, 104–105
Goldberg, David E. 2
Goodman, Andrew 54
Greek/Greekness 39–40, 43, 94–95
Grimke sisters (Sarah and Angelina) 54, 61–62
Guns N' Roses 34

Hailey, Alex 41
Hampton Morgan, Juliette 54

Index 113

Harlem 21–22
HBCUs (Historically Black Colleges and
    Universities) 6
Healy, Joseph 68
Heron, Scott Gill 15
Holiday, Billie 15
Horne, Lena 37
Houdini 27
Huerta, Dolores 52
human: interactions 3, 87, 91; suffering
    65–66, 87
humanity 41, 49, 51, 81, 92, 103

identity: concept 3; dual 79; individual
    91; race/racial 1–2, 4, 6, 20, 28,
    35, 43, 64, 66, 69, 96–97; social
    60; teaching 5
ideology 3, 41, 93, 104
immigrant 16, 39, 43, 52, 65, 68, 91, 93
immigration 2, 64, 86, 90
implicit bias 58, 60
India 13, 16–19, 21, 24, 75, 81
Indigenous *see* Native American
individualism 3
Industrial Revolution 65
inequality 2–3, 46–47, 68
institutional: discrimination 1, 35; racism
    3, 51, 63
insurrection 103
interracial 39, 42
intersectionality 3–4
intimidation 5

Jamaica 51, 67–68, 76
Jamila, Titi 15
jazz 15, 21, 40
Jeffersons, The 34
Jim Crow 50, 60, 89, 91
Joplin, Janis 40

Kardia, Diana B. 5
Kim, Janine Young 1
King, Martin Luther 31
King, Rodney 34
Ku Klux Klan 23, 27, 82

Latin Americans 2, 64–65, 88–89,
    93, 103
Latino 88–89, 103
Lay, Benjamin 54
Lebron, Lolita 51
LGBTQ 52
literature 29–30, 50, 67, 74, 95

Little, Malcolm *see* Malcolm X
Liuzzo, Viola 54
Loewen, James 53
Louverture, Toussaint 14
Lumumba, Patrice 15
lynching 50–51, 92

Malcolm X 35, 52
male: faculty 5; students 5, 21, 58,
    67, 77
Mariscal, Jorge 4
marriage, inter-racial 17, 39, 42
Martin, Trayvon 61, 104
Marx, Karl 41, 46
Marxist 67, 93
McIntosh, Peggy 93
McRae, Carmen 15
memories 15–17, 36, 67, 96
meritocracy 3, 47, 61, 67, 85
microaggression 5, 57
minority 55, 65
morals/morality 2, 62, 102
Morris, Monique W. 53
Morrison, Toni 41
Motley Crue 34
Mr. Ed (tv series) 35
Mr. Greenjeans (cartoon) 36
murder 19, 21, 51, 60–61, 92,
    102–104

Nancy Drew mystery 30–31
narcissist 30
narrative 7–8, 27, 51, 54, 64, 87
National Association for the
    Advancement of Colored
    Persons 104
Native American 2, 64–65, 88, 90
NCC *see* New Castle County
neoliberalism 1–2, 55; *see also* racial
    neoliberalism
New Castle County 19
Newark, Delaware 14, 21
Newsome, Bree 52
Nigeria 68, 94

Obama, Barack 1
Object of My Desire 34
objectivity 2, 4, 7, 64, 80, 95, 99, 109
Omi, Michael 46
oppression 15, 22, 32, 41, 54, 65,
    96, 99
optimism 50, 54, 79
outrage 32–33, 63, 78, 102

114   *Index*

Parks, Rosa 29
Parrillo, Vincent 68
Parsons, Albert 54
Pessar, Patricia 68
Peters, Donna-Marie 24, *25*, 43, 55, 80, 96–98
Pittman, Chavella 5
playground 27, 39
police brutality 1, 93
political: correctness 58, 103; economy 2, 35
political movements 2, 15, 103, 105
Porgy and Bess 37
postmodernism 7
power: authoritarian 43, 49, 92; Black 36, 39, 52; relationships 3; *see also* empower/empowerment
PowerPoint 50, 90
Presley, Elvis 15
pride 16, 99
Primarily White Institution 21, 75
private 2, 8, 26, 28–29, 103
profiling 20
protection 2, 36
proud 14, 29, 86, 99
push-back 57, 76, 80, 104
PWI *see* Primarily White Institution

race: identity 2, 4, 6, 13, 45, 59, 64, 70; neutrality 3, 68–70; relations 2, 64, 89; research 59; as taboo 58; White 41, 88, 94
Race Studies Courses: challenges 46–48; faculty experiences 55, 74, 84, 86, 96; faculty identity 1, 5–6, 99; research objectivity 7; subjectivity 6, 110
race-based inequalities 1, 3, 13, 91, 98
racial/racialized: consciousness 4; dominance 2, 13, 38, 97; identities 2–4, 13, 70, 96–97, 99–100; justice 6, 84, 103–104; subjectivity 2, 6, 99; subordination 2, 13
racialization 2–3, 6, 64, 70
racial subordination, not-white 2, 13
racism: institutionalized 15; public health 105; White 4, 61, 66
radical movements 62–63
Reinharz, Shulamit 7
representation 66–67, 69
resist 14, 16, 22, 35, 50, 54, 98

resistance: institutional 4, 6, 13, 15, 54; student 6, 62, 82, 98, 100
respect 7, 16, 27, 59
revolutionaries 15, 51, 53, 75
riot/rioting 32
Rivera, Sylvia 52
rock and roll 15, 40
Rockettes 15
Rogers Park (Chicago) 31
Roots (television mini-series) 33
Ross, Diana 15
Rothenberg, Paula 50
rules of race 43

sadness 32–33, 48, 67, 83, 98
Schwerner, Michael 54
Sea World 33
segregation 19, 50, 65, 81, 89–90, 92, 99
self-control 56, 78
self-determination (Kujichagulia) 13
Shakespeare, William 80
Shakur, Assata 14
silence 22, 32–33, 82–83, 96
Simone, Nina 15
Simpson, Nicole 42
Simpson, OJ 42
Smalls, Robert 62
social: construction theory 2–4, 6, 91; implications 1, 3, 74, 91, 95; interaction 3–4; meaning 3, 13
sociological: analysis 64; perspective 3, 46, 60, 89, 91
solidarity 1, 54
Springsteen, Bruce 15
Starpoint 34
State University, New York 41
stereotypes 58, 60, 65, 74, 77–78
Stevenson, Bryan 53
Stricker, Mary 31, *31*, 43, 60, 84, 96–98
student: body 68, 70; emotion 47–49, 55; engagement 46, 78; graduate 21, 39, 45, 87, 97; voices 56, 58–59
students: of color 6, 30 50, 60–61, 65, 87–89, 93–94, 104; White 6, 31, 32, 50, 60, 65, 75–76, 78
subjectivity 2, 4, 6–7, 64, 95
suburbs 25, 30
success: instructor 1, 92; reality of 66, 68, 92; student 49
Supremes, The 15
symbolic interactionism 3
systemic racism 4, 97, 99, 102, 105

Index 115

TA *see* Teaching Assistantship
teachers: commitment 16, 47, 54;
    evaluation 5; race identity 4
Teaching Assistantship 23, 75
teaching difficulties 46–48
teaching methods: emotionality 48, 66,
    94, 99; identity based 5, 45–46;
    lectures 23, 46, 50–51, 75,
    81; pop-up class 91; student
    involvement 50, 54, 81
teaching race 6, 46, 56, 74, 78;
    preparedness 75
Temple University 45, 75–76
Temptations, The 15
theorists 2, 46, 97
Third World History 16
Thomas, Vaso 39, *40*, 43, 66, 92, 97–98
Thomas theorem 3
tradition 7, 15, 50
trauma/traumatizing 39, 43, 48, 50, 81,
    83, 96, 100
triggers 48–49, 85
Trump, Donald J. 103–104
Truong, Kimberly (et al 2014) 5
TU *see* Temple University
Tubman, Harriet 18, 24
TUCC *see* Temple University Center City
Turner, Nat 14
Tyson, James Ian 54

UD *see* University of Delaware
UMASS *see* University of Massachusetts
UMBC *see* University of Maryland
uncertainty 14, 102
University of Delaware 20–21
University of Maryland 23
University of Massachusetts 15

Vandross, Luther 34
Vasey, Denmark 14
victims 32, 83, 106
Vietnam War 15–16, 29, 37
violence 14, 20–21, 33, 50, 76,
    96–97

Walensky, Rachelle P. 105
Walker, Alice 41
Wallace, George 29
Washington Heights 41, 68
Washington, Grover 40
Washington, Harriet A. 53
Wells, Ida B. 51, 62
White Anglo-Saxon Protestantism 2,
    62, 65
White feminism 39
Whiteness 14, 21–24, 35, 39, 41, 43, 75,
    88, 93
Whiteness-centered 46–47
White privilege 2, 56, 76, 93
White racial dominance 2, 13, 38, 97
White Shadow 33
White supremacy 32, 35, 60, 70, 85, 92,
    103–105
Wikipedia 37
Wilmington, Delaware 17–19, 24, 75
Winant, Howard 35, 46
woke/wokeness 104
women faculty of color 5–6
working-class 16, 19, 26, 31, 88
Wright, Mary C. 5

Young, Neil 40

Zimmerman, George 61, 104
Zinn, Howard 53

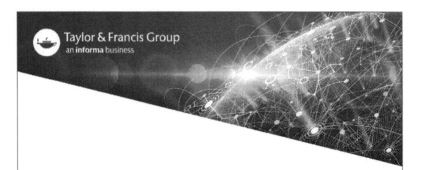

Printed in the United States
by Baker & Taylor Publisher Services